The
WORST-CASE SCENARIO
Book of Survival Questions

The
WORST-CASE SCENARIO
Book of Survival Questions

By Joshua Piven and David Borgenicht
Illustrations by Brenda Brown

CHRONICLE BOOKS

SAN FRANCISCO

Library of Congress Cataloging-in-Publication Data available.

ISBN: 0-8118-4539-7

Manufactured in Canada

Typeset in Adobe Caslon, Bundesbahn Pi, and Zapf Dingbats

Designed by Frances J. Soo Ping Chow
Illustrations by Brenda Brown

A **QUIRK** Book
Visit www.worstcasescenarios.com

Distributed in Canada by Raincoast Books
9050 Shaughnessy Street
Vancouver, British Columbia V6P 6E5

10 9 8 7 6 5 4 3 2 1

Chronicle Books LLC
85 Second Street
San Francisco, CA 94105
www.chroniclebooks.com

WARNING

When a life is imperiled or a dire situation is at hand, safe alternatives may not exist. To deal with the worst-case scenarios presented in this book, we highly recommend—insist, actually—that the best course of action is to consult a professionally trained expert. DO NOT ATTEMPT TO UNDERTAKE ANY OF THE ACTIVITIES DESCRIBED IN THIS BOOK YOURSELF, no matter how high you score on the Survival Aptitude Test or how many questions you answer correctly through the course of reading this book. But because highly trained professionals may not always be available when the safety of individuals is at risk, we have asked experts on various subjects to describe the techniques they might employ in those emergency situations. THE PUBLISHER, AUTHORS, AND EXPERTS DISCLAIM ANY LIABILITY from any injury that may result from the use, proper or improper, of the information contained in this book. We do not guarantee that the information contained herein is complete, safe, or accurate, nor should it be considered a substitute for your good judgment and common sense. Nothing in this book should be construed or interpreted to infringe on the rights of other persons or to violate criminal statutes: we urge you to obey all laws and respect all rights, including property rights, of others. And no cheating on the test.

—The Authors

INTRODUCTION

Do you have what it takes to survive life's sudden turns for the worse? Do you have the expertise, the skills, the presence of mind, the book smarts, and the street smarts it takes to survive when a life-threatening situation is at hand? And are you game enough to find out?

Since 1999, when the first *Worst-Case Scenario Survival Handbook* was published, we've instructed millions around the world about what to do when life takes a sudden turn for the worse. With each new book, as well as with the calendars, games, and TV series, and in speeches and demonstrations, we've endeavored again and again to teach our readers about the basic and specific skills you need to survive everything from natural disasters to animal attacks—in clear, step-by-step form, and with the help of experts in all matters of things.

Nearly every time we've spoken at bookstores, colleges, seminars, or corporate gatherings, we've given the crowd a "Survival Aptitude Test" testing their knowledge and expertise about what it takes to come out alive from a life-threatening situation.

Initially, this test started out as an icebreaker, to get the audience involved in the more serious material. But as we did more and more of these talks, we discovered that people found the test to be a valuable teaching tool. By using the test, we were able to address a large range of subjects in a very short amount of time, cover a wider range of problems and solutions, and quickly assess the audience's survival sense. (And also test their sense of humor.)

Now we've expanded and refined that test, and it's time for you to take it. In the safety of your own armchair or bathroom, you can determine your Survival Aptitude.

You probably know less than you think. And what you don't know now could save your life.

We've compiled this challenging collection of questions, answers, facts, and food for thought to assist you in assessing your skills—and in filling in the gaps.

This volume also offers a great way for you to test the mettle of your fellow adventurers and companions. Why assume that your best friend who wears a lot of expensive gear knows what to do when a crisis hits? Find out for sure. Using the questions (and answers) in this book, you can test and screen your friends and plan accordingly: By surrounding yourself with people who know how to survive, you're improving your own safety. And with the expert tips and lists of essential information, you can actually teach others how to be more prepared to deal with whatever may come along.

And on those rainy, cold nights when you don't really feel like going outside, *The Worst-Case Scenario Book of Survival Questions* provides excellent entertainment for groups of armchair survivalists as they test and rate each other's aptitude.

Experts not only provided the information contained herein. They also devised the best methods for testing your know-how. Within you'll find:

- **WORST-CASE STORY PROBLEMS**—High-impact, quick-response scenarios (with multiple-choice answers) that test your mental and physical abilities. The problems

are coded for level of difficulty, with four sharks
(🦈 🦈 🦈 🦈) being most difficult and one
shark (🦈) the easiest.

- **WORST-CASE DILEMMAS**—Tough choices and extreme situations with no single right answer.
- **WHAT'S WRONG WITH THIS PICTURE?**—Look and learn.
- **WHICH IS YOUR WORST CASE?**—Determine the limits of your tolerance and knowledge as more facts come into play.
- **WHAT'S THE WORST IT COULD BE?**—Identify the real danger you are facing.
- **ESSENTIAL INFORMATION LISTS**—Facts and advice you must know.
- **WORST-CASE FACT TICKER**—A constant flow of information to add to your survival expertise.
- **THE SURVIVAL APTITUDE TEST (SAT)**—At the end of the book, a formal test and grade. Are you a Master of Survival? A Ranger? A Scout? Or merely Bait?

No matter how you score, you'll learn. And the more you know, the better your chances of survival.

So stay calm, and think before you respond. And good luck.

You can begin NOW.

—The Authors

Worst-Case Scenario

SURVIVAL QUESTIONS

YOU HAVE FALLEN OUT OF YOUR RAFT INTO CLASS 5 WHITE-WATER RAPIDS, WITH HUGE BOULDERS QUICKLY APPROACHING.

Do you:

SWIM
Head for your raft and climb back in. (The raft will offer you more protection from the rocks.)

or

FLOAT
Lie on your back, face up, with your feet pointed downriver. (You might not make it back to your raft, and floating in proper position will protect you more than not being positioned at all.)

400,000 VIRUSES EXIST ON EARTH . . . SINCE 1950, THE MAJOR-

CAR FIRE

Level of Difficulty: 🦈🦈

You're driving along scenic State Route 64 in Arizona on a hot, sunny day. About 70 miles into your trip, just past Grandview Point, you notice the car's thermostat move into the red zone. Minutes later, you smell something burning and notice smoke coming through the dashboard vents. You turn the car off, and when you get out, you see flames coming from under the hood of the car. Do you:

(A) Open the hood and evaluate the situation

(B) Move away from the car and take cover

(C) Check under the car for a fuel leak

(D) Pour soda on the flames

(turn page for answer)

(B) Move away from the car and take cover

Though white smoke pouring from under the hood may indicate a cracked radiator and a coolant leak, the presence of flame and/or black or blue smoke indicates a very serious condition, possibly an electrical fire or a dangerous fuel or oil leak. Move away from the car and take cover in a ditch or behind a structure: If the car explodes, burning debris and gasoline may be thrown for yards in all directions. Never open the hood if you see flames, since you may be adding oxygen to the fire.

THE AVERAGE JULY TEMPERATURE IN DAVIS, ANTARCTICA, IS 1

WHICH IS
YOUR WORST CASE?

Facing a mountain lion
— or —
Facing a king cobra?

Be Aware
- A mountain lion can kill with a single bite to the throat.
- A king cobra's venom can stun your nervous system and stop your breathing.
- Much like domestic cats toying with a mouse, a mountain lion will kill for the sake of killing.
- A king cobra delivers more venom per bite than any other kind of cobra—as much as .2 fluid ounces, enough to kill 20 people.

WHAT'S THE WORST
IT COULD BE?

You are surfing in Maui and see a large wave far out to sea. Is it:

- the wake of a very large container ship

- the beginning swell of a 20-footer

- an approaching tsunami, which may be 50 to 100 feet high. The first tsunami may not be the largest in the series of waves, so immediately get as far inland as possible.

DUMPSTER DIVE

Level of Difficulty: 🦈🦈🦈

Working late one night, you hear a violent noise and possible gunshots in the hallway outside your office door. The door is the only safe way out of your office, but you don't want to open it to investigate or wait for someone dangerous to corner you inside. Your only other option is to climb out your fourth-story window. You quickly open the window and notice a Dumpster in the alley below. It is full of empty cardboard boxes. Hesitating for a moment, you watch as the door handle to your office turns. Do you:

(A) Leap out and as far away from the building as possible

(B) Jump straight down into the Dumpster, executing a three-quarter somersault to land on your back

(C) Jump straight down into the Dumpster, keeping your body vertical and landing on your feet

(D) Hang onto the window ledge by your fingertips until you believe it is safe to reenter your office

(turn page for answer)

NORTH AMERICA, INJECT A CHEMICAL INTO THEIR PREY THAT

ANSWER:

(B) Jump straight down into the Dumpster, executing a three-quarter somersault to land on your back

To survive your jump into the Dumpster unscathed, you must land on your back. Your body will naturally fold into a V when you land, and any other landing will break numerous bones. Do not leap far from the building, or your trajectory may cause you to miss your target.

EXPERT TIP

Do not jump into Dumpsters filled with bricks, construction debris, or other hard objects—try other means of egress.

TURNS THEIR INSIDES TO LIQUID . . . 1,198 PEOPLE WERE KILLED

Jump straight down.

*Tuck your head and bring your legs around,
executing a three-quarter somersault.*

Aim for the center of the Dumpster and land flat on your back.

RATS

- A rat can work its way through any opening larger than half a square inch.

- A rat can fall five stories without getting hurt.

- A rat can slip the skin off its tail and escape if caught.

- A rat will hiss or screech when threatened or attacking.

- Rats can mate 20 times a day and are in heat about every four to five days.

- The average female rat can have between four and seven litters per year.

- The average rat litter is 12 babies.

- A mother rat may eat her entire litter if she is malnourished.

- A rat may urinate as many as 80 times and defecate as many as 40 times a day.

- Rats spread typhoid, rat-bite fever, Weil's disease, salmonella, rabies, hantavirus, dysentery, trichinosis, Lassa fever, and bubonic plague, among other bacteria, viruses, and parasites.

TORPEDO . . . A BALL PYTHON CAN BE ROLLED ON THE GROUND

SUBWAY TRAIN APPROACHING

Level of Difficulty: ✦✦✦✦

While in Philadelphia, you head into the subway to take the El to City Hall. Bending down to tie your shoe on the platform, you are jostled by the crowd and lose your balance, falling down onto the tracks. You look down the tunnel and see a bright light, then hear an air horn. The train is approaching, and you do not have time to climb up to escape. To avoid being hit, do you:

(A) Lie down between the tracks

(B) Stand next to a pillar between two sets of tracks

(C) Stand flush with the sidewall

(D) Run up the tracks beyond the point where the train will stop

(turn page for answer)

WHEN IT IS FULLY COILED IN ITS DEFENSIVE "BALL" . . . ALFRED

(B) Stand next to a pillar between two sets of tracks

There should be enough clearance between the sets of tracks for you to stand safely; keep your arms flat against your sides. Do not stand next to a flat wall; there may not be enough clearance between the wall and the train. (If you must stand next to a wall, get in an alcove.) Avoid standing near or touching the electrified third rail. Lie down between the tracks only as a last resort. There may not be enough clearance, or the train may be dragging something that can injure you.

The gaps between pillars offer your best margin of safety.

EXPERT TIP

Avoid areas marked with red, white, or yellow paint stripes: These areas do not offer a safe margin of clearance.

NOBEL, NAMESAKE OF THE NOBEL PRIZE, PATENTED DYNAMITE IN

Parachute Problems

Level of Difficulty: 🦈🦈🦈🦈

It's your first skydiving trip. After packing, checking, and double-checking your main and reserve parachutes, you head up in the small plane with your instructor. When you're given the signal, you jump from the plane's open doorway. At the proper altitude, you pull your rip cord. Nothing happens. You pull the rip cord on your reserve parachute. Nothing happens. You look up, and you see your instructor diving toward you, having not yet deployed his chute. Do you:

(A) Aim for a swimming pool, lake, or other body of water

(B) Curl into a ball, protecting your head with your hands

(C) Wave your arms at your instructor, embrace your instructor with both your arms and legs, and hold on while he deploys his parachute

(D) Wave your arms at your instructor, hook your arms into your instructor's harness, and hold on while he deploys his parachute

(turn page for answer)

1867 . . . 1929 WAS THE MOST DEADLY YEAR FOR FLYING BASED

ANSWER:

(D) Wave your arms at your instructor, hook your arms into your instructor's harness, and hold on while he deploys his parachute

As long as your jumping companion has not yet deployed his parachute, you should be able to link up, put both of your arms through your instructor's harness, grab your own harness, and drift down under the canopy. However, two people under a parachute made for one may hit the ground hard, so be prepared for possible broken bones. Do not aim for a body of water, because if you are knocked unconscious you may drown. Never skydive alone.

Hook your arms into your companion's chest strap, up to the elbows, and grab hold of your own.

WHICH IS
YOUR WORST CASE?

Being stabbed
— or —
Being shot?

Be Aware
- Bullet wounds are smaller but may cause more severe internal injuries.
- Because a knife wound is larger, it has a greater chance of hitting a blood vessel.
- Bullets may ricochet in the body and injure organs away from the initial entry point.
- A large knife wound may require dozens of stitches.

THE BRAKES ON YOUR CAR HAVE FAILED, AND IT'S HEADING AT HIGH SPEED TOWARD THE EDGE OF A 20-FOOT DROP-OFF.

Do you:

JUMP

Leap from the car before it careens over the edge. (Your body will continue traveling in the direction and at the speed of the car.)

or

SWIM

Climb out of the car after it has hit the water and begins to sink. (Water pressure can make sealed windows extremely difficult to open under water.)

FATALITY FOR EVERY 1,000,000 MILES . . . YELLOWSTONE

BLACK WIDOW

Level of Difficulty: 🦈🦈

Before winter sets in, you decide to move your pile of cord-wood into a shed to shield it from the elements. Though it has been a wet summer and fall, the wood has been covered by a tarp and is generally dry. Near the bottom of the pile, you remove a piece of wood and see a spiderweb nearly a foot in diameter with a black spider at its outer edge. You examine the spider more closely and recognize it as a black widow. You know that female black windows are highly poisonous, while males are harmless. To determine if the spider is male or female, do you:

(A) Check for blue markings on its back

(B) Check for red or orange hourglass-shaped markings on the spider's abdomen

(C) Check for red spots and white bars on the spider's abdomen

(D) Check for a bull's-eye pattern on the spider's back

(turn page for answer)

NATIONAL PARK MAY BE A DORMANT SUPERVOLCANO . . .

(B) Check for red or orange hourglass-shaped markings on the spider's abdomen

An hourglass marking (two triangles facing each other) on the spider's abdomen indicates a dangerous female black widow. Though the colors may be yellowish, orange, or red, the presence of the hourglass always indicates a female; males are generally half the size of females and have red spots and white bars or lines radiating out to the sides of the abdomen.

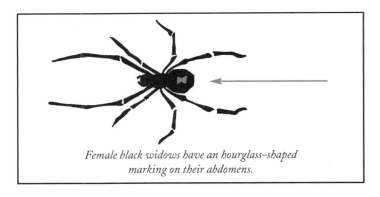

Female black widows have an hourglass-shaped marking on their abdomens.

EXPERT TIP

Though only 1 percent of female black widow bites actually result in death, the venom is poisonous and the spider should be considered dangerous. If you are bitten, seek medical attention.

SYNTHETIC MATERIALS MELT AT A LOWER TEMPERATURE THAN

FACE-TO-FACE WITH BEAR

Level of Difficulty: 🦈🦈

You live in a home on a large tract of land on the edge of a national forest. For the last three mornings, you've awakened to find your garbage cans tipped over and the bags of garbage shredded, with food scraps and trash strewn everywhere. You blame raccoons—you've had trouble with them getting into your garbage before. But this morning, as you are walking to the shed behind your house, you come face-to-face with the culprit, a small black bear. The two of you face each other, waiting to see who will make the first move. Do you:

(A) Climb a nearby tree and wait for the bear to leave

(B) Run the 100 yards back to the house

(C) Yell and wave your arms to scare the bear away

(D) Hold out your hands, palms facing outward, to show the bear that you are not afraid and that you mean it no harm

(turn page for answer)

NATURAL FIBERS BURN . . . SLURRED SPEECH IS A SIGN OF

(C) **Yell and wave your arms to scare the bear away**

Hold your ground and make enough noise and motion to scare the bear away; running may only cause it to chase you, and bears can run as fast as horses. Bears habituated to the presence of humans and human garbage may be more difficult to scare away. If you cannot scare the bear away, back off very slowly and get inside.

Mother bears will actively defend their cubs,
so if you see a bear cub, assume a full-grown bear is nearby.

BEARS

- Bears can run as fast as 40 mph, even uphill.

- Bears have been known to aggressively attack menstruating women.

- Bears are extremely strong. They can tear cars apart looking for food.

- The most dangerous bears of any species are females defending cubs, bears habituated to human food, and bears defending a fresh kill.

- Bears defend "personal space," which may be a few meters or a few hundred meters, depending on the bear.

- Kodiak bears are the largest of the bear species, weighing up to 1,500 pounds and standing as tall as 10 feet.

- A female black bear's natural defense is to chase her cubs up a tree and defend them from the base.

- Bears are excellent swimmers, and can easily reach campsites on islands.

- All bears can climb trees.

- Black bears are better tree climbers than grizzly bears.

ANIMAL, ABLE TO RUN 70 MPH . . . PEOPLE LOOK TO THE LEFT

WHICH IS
YOUR WORST CASE?

Falling through ice
while hiking
— or —
Falling through ice
while driving in a car?

Be Aware
- A car will sink, while a person can float.
- The car offers at least some temporary protection from the freezing water.
- If you fall through the ice, you may be able to haul yourself back out.
- The car will allow you more time to plan your escape.

MARKING THE TRAIL

Level of Difficulty: ◂━ ◂━ ◂

You are on a tour of Braulio Carillo National Park near San José, Costa Rica. You are separated from the group and have lost your way. You shout for help, but hear no reply. You will have to make your own way out. You decide to mark your trail in case you need to backtrack—you don't want to wander around in circles. To mark your path, do you:

(A) Leave a trail of breadcrumbs

(B) Turn over leaves and other vegetation

(C) Line your trail with sticks set end to end

(D) Make blazes on trees with chalk or a sharp rock

(turn page for answer)

(B) **Turn over leaves and other vegetation**

The best way to mark a trail in heavy jungle or rain forest is to turn over leaves to reveal their bright undersides; this will leave an easy-to-follow path should you need to reverse course. Do not leave a trail of food: It will be eaten by animals. Chalk may be washed off during heavy rains, and stone marks on tree trunks may be difficult to see. Setting sticks end to end is time consuming, and they may become indistinguishable from other ground cover.

EXPERT TIP

In dense jungle, you may have to clear a path by cutting away at vegetation. Chop downwards and as low as possible on both sides of the stems so that the plants fall away from your path rather than across it.

ABOVE THE TIMBERLINE ARE RISKY PLACES TO BE DURING A

WHAT'S WRONG
WITH THIS PICTURE?

(turn page for answer)

THUNDERSTORM . . . TSUNAMIS CAUSE DAMAGE WHEN WAVES

ANSWER:

The person is trying to break down a door by ramming it with his shoulder.

Slamming into a locked door with your shoulder is unlikely to break down the door and could result in injury to your shoulder or a broken arm. Further, if the door is a flimsy hollow-core door, you may fly right through it, causing severe lacerations from splintered wood.

THE RIGHT WAY

Make one (or several) well-placed kicks just above the door handle, in the area of the lock. This action will either splinter the door frame or separate the locking mechanism from the door, allowing you to gain entry. Alternatively, if the hinges of the door are exposed, you can remove the hinge pins using a flat-blade screwdriver and gain entry from the side opposite the lock.

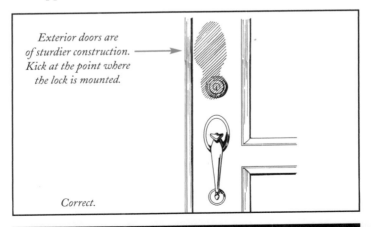

Exterior doors are of sturdier construction. Kick at the point where the lock is mounted.

Correct.

MOVE FROM DEEPER WATER TO SHALLOWER WATER . . .

CORRUPT BORDER OFFICIAL

Level of Difficulty:

You are crossing the border between two countries known for corrupt and greedy border officials. One guard claims that your papers are not in order and warns that you are in for a night in jail before things will be "straightened out" in the morning. Do you:

(A) Ask to call your country's embassy

(B) Ask him how large a bribe he requires

(C) Demand to speak to his superior

(D) Suggest that you will pay a fine directly to him

(turn page for answer)

LIGHTNING IS ESTIMATED AT 50,000 DEGREES FAHRENHEIT,

(D) **Suggest that you pay a fine directly to him**

Never blatantly offer a bribe: If you have misunderstood the official's intentions, you may get yourself into more trouble. Avoid getting angry and raising your voice. Stay calm and be friendly but slightly aloof. Consider offering a "donation" to the force's uniform fund or a "sample" of any desirable goods (wine, food, cigarettes) you are carrying.

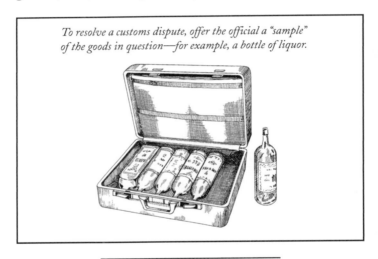

To resolve a customs dispute, offer the official a "sample" of the goods in question—for example, a bottle of liquor.

EXPERT TIP

Carry only a small amount of cash in your wallet; if you need to pay cash, you will avoid showing the official your entire wad.

HOTTER THAN THE SURFACE OF THE SUN . . . LIGHTNING STRIKE

WHAT'S THE WORST
IT COULD BE?

While driving in your car, you hear a loud, sustained roar. Is it:

• a jet passing overhead

• thunder

• a tornado approaching your location. A car is one of the most dangerous places to be during a tornado. Get into the basement of a nearby home, stop the car and lie in a ditch, or drive away as fast as you can, at a right angle to the approaching tornado.

YOU ARE CAUGHT IN AN AUTO TUNNEL FIRE.

Do you:

WAIT

Remain in your car and wait for emergency crews to arrive and help you exit the tunnel safely. (The longer you stay in the tunnel, the greater the odds that you will be trapped if it collapses.)

or

LEAVE

Abandon your car and walk through the tunnel until you find an emergency exit. (You may become disoriented in the smoke and walk toward the fire rather than away from it.)

TOUCHED SAFELY . . . MOSS GROWS ON ALL SIDES OF A TREE,

WHICH IS
YOUR WORST CASE?

Jumping from a bridge
into a river

— or —

Going over a waterfall?

Be Aware
- You could break your legs or your back when you hit the water in the river.
- The pressure of the waterfall may prevent you from surfacing.
- The river may be very shallow.
- You could injure yourself on rocks at the bottom of the waterfall.

WHILE SNOWMOBILING YOU SEE THAT AN AVALANCHE IS BEGINNING HIGH ABOVE YOU.

Do you:

ESCAPE

Try to outrun the approaching snow on your snowmobile. (You are more likely to be injured if you are overcome while on the vehicle.)

or

STOP

Abandon your vehicle and try to stay on top of the snow. (You may be able to avoid the snow entirely by remaining on the vehicle and speeding away at the proper angle.)

NOT JUST THE NORTH SIDE . . . BURNING TIRES CREATE THICK

WHAT'S THE WORST
IT COULD BE?

You are in the Caribbean, leisurely swimming apart from your group of friends, and you feel a rough bump against your leg. Is it:

- a sea turtle

- a curious barracuda

- a tiger shark about to attack using the "bump and bite" technique, in which the shark circles and bumps its victim prior to attacking. With this type of attack, repeat bites are common, and injuries sustained are usually quite severe and even fatal.

RADIATION

- People who live in high elevations are exposed to higher levels of cosmic radiation.

- As many as 8,000 people died as a result of the April 26, 1986, Chernobyl accident and its cleanup; 4.9 million people were estimated to have been exposed to radiation.

- The average American receives about 300 millirems of radiation per year.

- A five-hour plane ride will lead to 3 millirems of radiation exposure.

- A lethal dose of radiation is between 450,000 and 600,000 millirems when the entire body is exposed.

- A car or building will provide some level of radiation protection.

- Radioactive alpha particles can be blocked with a sheet of paper.

- Radioactive neutrons can travel long distances in the air but can be blocked with water or concrete.

- Half of all people with cancer are treated with radiation.

- There is no effective treatment for radiation sickness.

WAS NAMED THE FIRST EAGLE SCOUT IN AUGUST 1912 . . . A

STUCK IN QUICKSAND

Level of Difficulty: ◆◆◆

You've finally decided to pay a visit to your eccentric Uncle Elroy, who lives in a remote cabin in marshy backwater far off the main road. While hiking out to the cabin, you pick up a long, straight branch to use as a walking stick. A few minutes later, suddenly and without warning, you feel yourself sinking into the damp ground. Struggling to pull your feet free, you find to your dismay that the more you pull, the harder it is to escape. You're stuck in quicksand. Do you:

(A) Yell for help, even though there is little chance anyone will hear your cries

(B) Move your legs in a swift running motion in an attempt to escape

(C) Place your walking stick under your hips, lie on your back, and float out of the quicksand

(D) Place your stick vertically in the quicksand until you feel solid ground below, then attempt to hike out

(turn page for answer)

ANSWER:

(C) Place your walking stick under your hips, lie on your back, and float out of the quicksand

You are more buoyant in quicksand than you are in water, so floating out is the best way to escape its clutches. Spread your arms and legs out to distribute your weight, but move slowly: The viscosity of quicksand increases with shearing—the more you move, the thicker the quicksand and the harder it is to move. Move slowly and carefully to reduce the amount of resistance you will face.

Use the walking stick to put your back into a floating position.

Place the stick at a right angle from your spine to keep your hips afloat.

THE "PLEASE MAKE UP MY ROOM" DOOR HANGER IN HOTELS

44.

WHICH IS
YOUR WORST CASE?

Jumping out of a car going 40 mph

— or —

**Jumping off a motorcycle
going 60 mph?**

Be Aware

- In the car, you're unlikely to be wearing protective gear.
- The motorcycle is moving faster.
- It may be harder to get clear of the car.
- A motorcycle is an unstable jumping-off point.

WHAT'S THE WORST
IT COULD BE?

You are walking down a deserted street on your way to dinner and you see a shadow moving behind you in the corner of your eye. Is it:

• another passerby

• a stray dog

• a mugger about to attack you from behind. Do not resist unless your life is in danger—your possessions aren't worth it. However, if a mugger means to do you harm, attack vital areas of your assailant's body, such as eyes, groin, throat, and knees.

SWORD FIGHT

Level of Difficulty: ✦ ✦ ✦ ✦

On a trip to a local Renaissance fair, your friends encourage you to participate in a mock sword fight with one of the fair's expert swordsmen. It's only after you are in the ring with your fencing foil you realize your opponent takes this very seriously. Well over six feet tall and dressed in full chain mail, he is coming straight at you with his foil over his head. Do you:

(A) Move in close, keeping your sword above your head and parallel to the ground

(B) Take a step back and try to duck the blow

(C) Keep your sword in a vertical position and parry the blow to the side

(D) Step back and swing the sword like a bat to hit him in the knees

(turn page for answer)

ANSWER:

(A) **Move in close, keeping your sword above your head and parallel to the ground**

Though it's probably against your instincts, moving in close will help to lessen the force of the blow, because your opponent will not have achieved full extension and thrust. Absorb the blow in the center of your sword, not on the end, and "punch" out with your counter blow, which may catch your opponent off guard.

EXPERT TIP

Always carry your sword in the "ready" position—held in front of you, with both hands, and perpendicular to the ground. With this method you can move the sword side to side and up and down easily, blocking and landing blows in all directions by moving your arms. Picture a doorway—you should be able to move the sword in any direction and quickly hit any edge of the door frame.

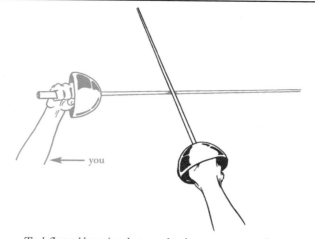

*To deflect a blow aimed at your head, move your sword
parallel to the ground and above you.*

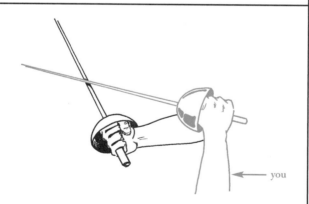

*Wait for your attacker to make a mistake before you attack.
Deflecting a blow to the side will throw your opponent off balance.*

WHILE YOU ARE IN KANSAS, YOU HEAR ON THE NEWS THAT A TORNADO IS APPROACHING YOUR MOBILE HOME.

Do you:

FLEE TO STURDIER SHELTER

Run to the nearest building with a basement and take shelter inside until the tornado has passed. (You risk getting caught in the open before you reach shelter.)

or

LIE DOWN IN A DITCH

Run outside and lie flat in a nearby ditch or culvert, and cover your head with your arms. (A basement offers more protection than a ditch.)

PUBLISHED *ROBINSON CRUSOE* IN 1719 . . . OLD, BLUE-COLORED

SHOOT-OUT

Level of Difficulty: 🦈 🦈

While you are on a long-awaited tropical vacation, the government of the small island nation you are visiting is toppled by a coup d'état. There is panic, rioting, and gunfire in the streets. You pick up the telephone in your hotel room to call your embassy, but the phone is dead. You will have to reach the embassy on foot. As you leave the hotel and move into the street, you see a gang of armed thugs on one side of you and uniformed military officers on the other. The two groups raise their guns to battle, and you are in the crossfire. Do you:

(A) Lie flat in the street, next to the curb

(B) Crouch down behind the tire of a nearby parked car

(C) Run into a nearby building

(D) Stand in place and wave a white handkerchief

(turn page for answer)

SEA ICE HAS LESS SALT THAN NEW SEA ICE . . . FRAN PHIPPS

ANSWER:

(A) **Lie flat in the street, next to the curb**

If you are not the primary target of the shooters, get as low as possible to get out of the line of fire. Do not crouch, and do not hide behind a car tire: High-caliber bullets can easily penetrate a tire or sheet metal, and by crouching you may be mistaken for a shooter. Running away from the shooters may only draw their attention and lead them to fire on you by mistake. When the opportunity presents itself, turn a corner and use back streets to make your way to safety.

EXPERT TIP

Always carry a street map in an unknown city.

WHICH IS
YOUR WORST CASE?

Being on a sinking ship in the
North Atlantic
— or —
Being lost in the Sahara?

Be Aware

- An average person can remain conscious for only about an hour in water 40°F.
- Most people cannot survive more than three days without drinking water.
- Prolonged exposure to salt water can cause skin lesions, which are prone to infection.
- The Sahara can reach more than 130°F during the day, increasing the risk of heatstroke.

WHAT'S THE WORST
IT COULD BE?

While on a boating expedition on the Amazon, you gaze over the side of your craft and notice dozens of long objects in the water. Are they:

• sticks

• snakes

• electric eels capable of producing 500 volts of electricity, enough voltage to kill a person.

TRAPPED IN A WELL

Level of Difficulty: 🦈🦈🦈

While gazing into a well to see if it contains any water, you lose your footing and fall in. Amazingly, you are scratched and scraped but otherwise uninjured from the fall. The well is empty, but you are at least 30 feet below ground. With no rope and no one above to hear your cries for help, you must climb out. Do you:

(A) Climb straight up one side, hand over hand

(B) Assume a spread-eagle position with arms and legs outstretched, feet down

(C) Keep your back straight against one side and your legs straight out in an L

(D) Arch your back across the well, reaching to the far side with your hands

(turn page for answer)

AND ATTACK FOR A DISTANCE OF 150 YARDS . . . RUBBER

(C) **Keep your back straight against one side and your legs straight out in an L**

In this position, you can place your hands under your buttocks and put pressure against the wall. Then, by bending one leg, put the sole of your foot under your hand and push up. Repeat the process, alternating legs, until you have climbed out of the well.

Place your back against one wall and your hands and feet against the other.

Using even pressure to maintain traction, place your hands below your rear.

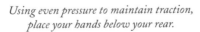

GLOVES WILL NOT OFFER PROTECTION WHEN YOU ATTEMPT TO

*Take one foot off the wall and
place it under your rear.*

*Push up with your hands.
Repeat steps 1 through 4.*

WHICH IS
YOUR WORST CASE?

Suffering a severe case of poison ivy

— or —

Suffering an extreme sunburn?

Be Aware

- Itching caused by the allergic reaction to poison ivy can last for weeks.
- Severe sunburn increases the chance of skin cancer.
- The rash caused by poison ivy can cause scarring.
- Sunburn can cause fever and swelling of the skin, release toxins, and cause the skin to blister, itch, and peel.

WHAT'S WRONG
WITH THIS PICTURE?

(turn page for answer)

SOURCE . . . DO NOT ATTEMPT TO SWIM IN FRIGID WATER

ANSWER:

The man is standing under a lone tree during a lightning storm.

The tree is the tallest structure in the area, making it a prime target for a lightning strike. If the tree is hit, the lightning current may flashover, or jump, from the tree to the man. It could also cause the tree to explode, and the man will be hurt by careening wood fragments.

THE RIGHT WAY

If you are caught in an open space during a lightning storm, the best way to avoid being struck is to make yourself into the smallest target possible. Squat on the balls of your feet, place your hands over your ears, and lower your head between your knees. Stay on the balls of your feet to minimize contact with the ground. Do not crouch with your hands on the ground, and do not lie flat.

Correct.

UNLESS YOU ARE CERTAIN YOU CAN GET OUT QUICKLY . . .

FALL THROUGH
SIDEWALK GRATE

Level of Difficulty: 🦈 🦈 🦈

While running down Fifth Avenue in Manhattan to catch a bus, you step on a flimsy yellow sidewalk grate and fall straight down, landing on your rear end at the bottom of a dark shaft. Dazed but unhurt, you look around and take stock. You appear to be in a subway tunnel. Though it is dark, you can see light above you from where you fell through the grate. To escape, do you:

(A) Walk down the tunnel to find the nearest station

(B) Use your hands to search the area for a ladder going up to the sidewalk

(C) Use your cell phone to call for help

(D) Yell for assistance

(turn page for answer)

LEECHES ARE ATTRACTED TO VIBRATION AND BODY HEAT . . .

ANSWER:

(B) Use your hands to search the area for a ladder going up to the sidewalk

Yellow sidewalk grates generally denote an emergency exit from a subway tunnel below. There should be a ladder that will take you back to the surface. Avoid wandering along subway tracks (you may be hit by a train). Though you may still have a cell phone signal, it will take time for rescuers to locate you. Yelling probably won't get you much attention in the noise of the city.

HYDRAULIC ELEVATORS ARE MORE LIKELY TO FALL THAN CABLE

WHICH IS
YOUR WORST CASE?

Having frostbitten fingers
— or —
Having badly burned fingers?

Be Aware
- Frostbitten areas may need to be amputated if they are not rewarmed promptly.
- Burns—even superficial burns—can become severely infected, and the infection can quickly spread.
- Frostbitten digits are extremely painful when rewarmed.
- Burns may require months or years of recovery time.

WHAT'S THE WORST
IT COULD BE?

You are walking through Tokyo and feel the ground begin to shake and roll. Is it:

• the vibration from a nearby road crew

• a passing 18-wheeler

• "the Big One" about to topple high-rise buildings. Move away from buildings, power lines, chimneys, and anything that might fall on you. Be prepared for aftershocks—another quake, larger or smaller, may follow.

MOB OF KANGAROOS

Level of Difficulty: 🦈 🦈

During a train trip through Australia's southern desert, you've experienced wonderful scenery and long vistas. At a short layover, the conductor suggests that passengers can get out and take pictures if they choose. You get off the train and wander onto the sandy soil, only to come face-to-face with a mob of seven or eight kangaroos. As you slowly approach for a close-up photo, one kangaroo begins thumping his large feet. Do you:

(A) Continue approaching without showing fear

(B) Move away quickly so you are more than ten feet from the closest kangaroo

(C) Back away slowly

(D) Stand up straight and tall and open your coat wide to make yourself seem larger

(turn page for answer)

(C) **Back away slowly**

Kangaroos are herbivores and will rarely attack any animal, including humans. However, some male kangaroos may be over 7 feet tall and weigh hundreds of pounds, and may charge if cornered or threatened. Thumping indicates that the kangaroo is alerting group members to danger. If a kangaroo attacks, there is no truly safe distance: Large kangaroos can jump 20 feet or more and travel as fast as 40 mph. If you notice thumping, move back slowly and seek shelter.

EXPERT TIP

Fences are not a suitable kangaroo deterrent, as they easily can be jumped by larger kangaroos.

USEFUL FOR MAKING AN EMERGENCY SHELTER . . . INEXPERI-

*Kangaroos alert others in their mob to danger
by thumping their feet.*

ENCED RIDERS SHOULD TIE A HORSE'S REINS TOGETHER SO THE

WHICH IS
YOUR WORST CASE?

**Removing a tick
from your arm
— or —
Removing a leech
from your leg?**

Be Aware
- Leeches can be very difficult to remove.
- Ticks can carry Lyme disease, which can cause
  muscle pain; meningitis; numbness, tingling, and
  burning in the extremities; severe pain; and
  extreme and incapacitating fatigue.
- Bacteria from a leech's digestive system can spread
  into your open wound, causing infection.
- Ticks can carry Rocky Mountain spotted fever,
  which can cause kidney failure and death if not
  treated promptly.

DITCHING A MOTORCYCLE

Level of Difficulty: 🦈 🦈 🦈

You are about to leap from your burning motorcycle to your friend's car that is traveling beside you. Your friend is matching your speed of 45 mph and signaling for you to jump. Do you:

(A) Leap onto the hood and hold the windshield

(B) Throw yourself onto the roof and grab the roof rack

(C) Climb through an open front passenger window

(D) Wait for your friend to open the door

(turn page for answer)

REINS DO NOT FALL PAST THE HORSE'S NECK AND CAUSE IT TO

ANSWER:

(C) **Climb through an open front passenger window**

Your best chance of survival is to grab the inside roof handle of the front seat, then swing your body through the window opening. The vehicles should be on a long, straight stretch of road and should not be moving faster than 60 mph. As soon as you have made the transfer, the driver of the car should swerve away from the path of the driverless motorcycle to avoid running over it and crashing.

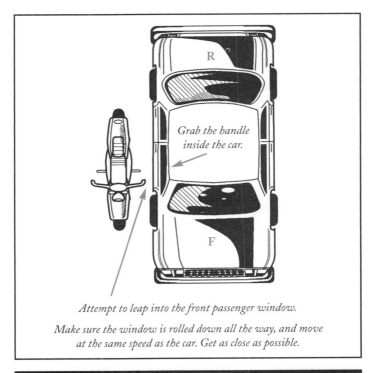

Grab the handle inside the car.

Attempt to leap into the front passenger window.

Make sure the window is rolled down all the way, and move at the same speed as the car. Get as close as possible.

Trapped by Storm

Level of Difficulty: 🦈

You have hiked alone high into the mountains on a cool autumn day. After a picnic lunch, you debate turning back but decide to continue ahead a bit farther. You notice clouds gathering to the west, and within minutes, a freak fall storm has barreled in. The temperature drops, it gets dark, and you lose your way in what starts as a downpour but quickly turns to snow. You are lucky enough to find a large overhanging rock under which you wait out the storm. An hour later, when the storm has passed, you can't find the trail under the fresh snow to hike back out. You are hopelessly lost. You decide to build a signal fire for your rescuers. Do you:

(A) Hike down into a valley to build the fire

(B) Hike up to a nearby peak to build the fire

(C) Wait until night and then build the fire

(D) Stay put and build the fire under the overhanging rock

(turn page for answer)

(B) Hike up to a nearby peak to build the fire

Rescuers are most likely to spot smoke from a signal fire built during the day on a peak, not deep in a valley. However, do not hike long distances or you risk getting cold, tired, and hypothermic. Do not build a fire for signaling at night, when the smoke is impossible to see.

If you are lost in the mountains, do not hike aimlessly and without direction: The closer you are to your original path, the more likely rescuers are to find you.

EXPERT TIP

Before hiking in the wilderness, especially if you're hiking alone, always tell someone where you are going and when you expect to return.

THE WILDERNESS

- ✪ Always carry a lighter or waterproof matches and clothes-dryer lint for starting fires.

- ✪ Always tell at least one person where you are going and when you will be back.

- ✪ Carry a pocketknife and a compass.

- ✪ Check your cell phone battery for a full charge, and carry a spare.

- ✪ Bring a map or use a global positioning system receiver to determine your location.

- ✪ Put heavier items in the center of your pack, close to your back.

- ✪ Carry zip-closure plastic bags to protect nonwaterproof items.

- ✪ Bring iodine tablets to purify water.

- ✪ Pack sunscreen, a brimmed hat, and sunglasses, even for cold weather environments.

- ✪ Wear waterproof shoes and bring extra socks.

SHOULD BE SCRAPED, NOT PULLED, FROM THE SKIN . . . ICE IS

WHICH IS
YOUR WORST CASE?

Being bitten by a raccoon
— or —
Being bitten by a vampire bat?

Be Aware

- Raccoons frequently carry rabies.
- A vampire bat may feed on its victim's blood for 30 minutes or more.
- Raccoons have 40 teeth and razor-sharp claws.
- A vampire bat's saliva contains a chemical that prevents blood from clotting, and another that numbs an animal's (or human's) skin, preventing it from feeling the bite and waking up.

OVER THE FALLS

Level of Difficulty: 🦈 🦈 🦈

What was supposed to be a modestly challenging white-water rafting trip in New Zealand has turned into a Class 5 nightmare: Heavy rains have made the trip treacherous, and the mighty 21-foot Tutea Falls await you just downriver. As you follow your guide's advice and check to make sure your helmet and life jacket are secure, you accidentally slip and fall from the raft. With the raft moving away from you and the falls quickly approaching, do you:

(A) Try to swim back to the raft

(B) Try to swim to shore

(C) Prepare to go over the falls head-first

(D) Prepare to go over the falls feet-first

(turn page for answer)

(D) **Prepare to go over the falls feet-first**

In a rapidly moving river, swimming back to a raft or to shore will be very difficult. Before you go over a waterfall, float on your back with your feet together and pointing downriver. In this position, you will hit any rocks or other obstructions in the river with your feet and legs, not your head and torso.

EXPERT TIP

As you go over the falls, put your arms over your head to protect it. After you hit the water, begin swimming out and away from the falling water and up to the surface as soon as possible. If you do not swim away from the base of the waterfall, the water pressure may hold you under and cause you to drown.

CARS WILL ROLL SIDE-OVER-SIDE ON ANY SLOPE GREATER THAN

Go over the falls feet-first, covering your head.

30 DEGREES . . . NITROGLYCERIN EXPLODES IN AIR WHEN HEATED

WHAT'S THE WORST
IT COULD BE?

You are in a small plane and notice the pilot slumped over the controls, and he does not respond when you try to get his attention. Is it:

• nap time

• cocktail time

• the pilot is unconscious or dead. You will have to take over. Tune the radio to 121.5 (the emergency channel), give your plane's call numbers and destination, describe your situation, and ask for someone to talk you through an emergency landing.

SPIN OUT

During a winter visit to Lake Edwards, Minnesota, for some competitive ice fishing, you are caught in a bad snow and ice storm. You pull into a gas station for a break from the storm, and an attendant looks at your car and laughs, saying that you'll probably crash within minutes in your rear-wheel-drive rental vehicle unless you do which of the following quick fixes:

(A) Buy a set of new tires

(B) Put two 50-pound sandbags in the trunk

(C) Fill up the tank with gas

(D) Fill the tires up with air

(turn page for answer)

EST RECORDED TEMPERATURE WAS -128.6 DEGREES FAHRENHEIT

(B) Put two 50-pound sandbags in the trunk

Rear-wheel-drive cars tend to skid on snow and ice because there is very little weight above the wheels with the power. To compensate, place one 50-pound bag of sand (garden stones and kitty litter also work) over each rear wheel to increase traction.

EXPERT TIPS

If you are trapped in your car during a blizzard:

- Stay in the car. Do not walk to find assistance unless help is visible within 100 yards. You may become lost or disoriented in the blowing and drifting snow.
- Hang a brightly colored cloth from the door handle or antenna and raise the hood.
- Turn on the engine for about 10 minutes each hour, and turn on the heater when the engine is running.
- To guard against carbon monoxide poisoning, open a downwind window slightly for ventilation and keep the exhaust pipe clear of snow.
- Do minor exercises to keep up circulation, but do not overexert yourself. Cold weather puts added strain on the body.

AT VOSTOK STATION, ANTARCTICA, ON JULY 21, 1983 . . .

YOU ARE RIDING ON AN OUT-OF-CONTROL SLED DOWN A MOUNTAINSIDE, AND YOU SEE A CREVASSE GAPING AHEAD.

Do you:

JUMP

Use the momentum built up in your downhill slide to jump over the crevasse on the sled. (The sled might not have the momentum to make it to the other side of the crevasse.)

or

BAIL OUT

Abandon the sled—jump off before you get to the crevasse. (If you land incorrectly, jumping from the sled may cause severe injury.)

GRIZZLY BEARS CAN RUN 30 MPH . . . THE WORLD HEALTH

WHICH IS
YOUR WORST CASE?

Walking across a minefield
— or —
Running from someone with a gun?

Be Aware
- Mines are difficult to see until you're on top of them.
- A gunman may outrun you.
- A land mine is designed to inflict maximum suffering, not to kill.
- A single bullet wound can kill you instantly.

WHAT'S WRONG
WITH THIS PICTURE?

(turn page for answer)

ORGANIZATION REPORTS 1,000 TO 3,000 CASES OF BUBONIC

ANSWER:
The person is attempting to fight off a shark by punching it in the jaw.

The jaw or snout is not the most sensitive part of a shark, and is not the best place to attack if you are fighting back. In addition, you may miss and end up with your hand in the shark's mouth.

THE RIGHT WAY

To fight back, attack the shark's eyes or gills with quick, sharp blows, preferably with an implement (spear, probe, camera), but even with your fists if they are your only weapons. In general, sharks are less likely to follow through with an attack if they feel their prey is not defenseless.

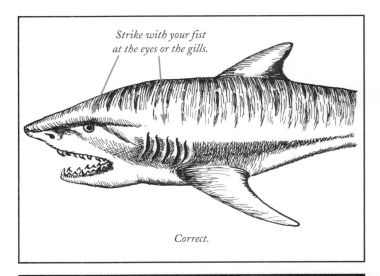

Strike with your fist at the eyes or the gills.

Correct.

ABANDON SHIP

Level of Difficulty: 🦈 🦈 🦈

You are the captain of your own 32-foot sailboat, sailing to the Grenadines. Though you've been warned that the passage through the Leeward Islands is treacherous, you try your luck and forge ahead, only to end up crashing the boat into a reef. As the boat begins to take on water, you have a decision to make: When should you abandon the boat for your life raft? You try to remember the old sailor's adage. Is it:

(A) "Always step up into your life raft"

(B) "Always get into your life raft before you need to"

(C) "If the raft is floating, the boat is sinking"

(D) "Good sailors don't rely on life rafts"

(turn page for answer)

SKIERS . . . TROPICAL CENTIPEDES GROW TO 11 INCHES LONG

ANSWER:

(A) **"Always step up into your life raft"**

The point of the adage is that you are better off with a boat—even one that is sinking—than on a life raft. Thus, your boat should be under water before you climb into your raft. Your boat will have an emergency transmitter that alerts the Coast Guard to your position. The farther you are from the position of your sunken vessel, the more difficult it will be for anyone to find you.

EXPERT TIP

If you have no choice but to move to your life raft, put on warm wool clothing, including a hat and gloves, and wrap a towel around your neck. The clothes will help prevent exposure to the cold water—a person can develop hypothermia within seven hours even in water that is 60 to 70°F.

TAXI BIRTH

Level of Difficulty: ◆◆◆

On a trip to China, you share a taxi from the airport into Shanghai with a very pregnant stranger. As the taxi sits in a major traffic jam on the highway into the city, the woman's water breaks and she begins to experience painful contractions. You both ask the taxi driver to take you to the hospital, but neither of you speak his dialect and you are unsure of whether he understands the situation. You may have to deliver the baby in the back of the cab. Is the first thing you do:

(A) Cover the seat of the cab with clean shirts from your suitcase

(B) Time the contractions from the beginning of one to the beginning of the next

(C) Time the contractions from the end of one to the beginning of the next

(D) Clean your hands using toothpaste if no other disinfectant is available

(turn page for answer)

KEY WEST TO THE MAINLAND WAS DESTROYED BY A HURRICANE

(B) Time the contractions from the beginning of one to the beginning of the next

The water breaking is not a reliable sign that birth is imminent, only that it will probably occur within 24 hours. The timing of the contractions is a better predictor, though babies are unpredictable and will not come out of the womb until they are ready. For first-time mothers, when contractions are 3 to 5 minutes apart and last 40 to 90 seconds in duration, the labor is probably real.

EXPERT TIPS

- Once you've determined that the baby is on the way, spread clean, dry towels, a clean shirt, or something similar to prepare for the delivery.
- As the baby moves out of the womb, its head—the biggest part of its body—will open the cervix so the rest of it can pass through. As the baby moves through the birth canal, guide it out by supporting the head and then the body.
- When the baby is out of the mother, dry it off and keep it warm. If necessary, clear any fluid out of the baby's mouth with your fingers.
- Take a piece of string—a shoelace works well—and tie off the umbilical cord several inches from the baby. It is not necessary to cut the umbilical cord unless you are several hours away from the hospital.

IN 1935 . . . THE FIRST CLIMBING PARTY TO REACH THE SUMMIT

*As the baby moves through the birth canal,
guide it out by supporting the head.*

*Support the body as it moves out. Do not slap its behind
to make it cry; the baby will breathe on its own.*

*After you have dried off the baby, tie the umbilical cord with a shoelace
or a piece of string several inches from the body. Leave the cord alone
until the baby gets to the hospital.*

OF THE MATTERHORN (14,692 FEET HIGH) LOST FOUR CLIMBERS

WHICH IS
YOUR WORST CASE?

**A hostile encounter
with a vulture
— or —
A hostile encounter
with a swarm of bees?**

Be Aware

- Each bee can sting only once.
- A vulture can projectile vomit partially digested carrion when it feels threatened.
- Even for those not allergic to bees, it is possible to be stung to death by many bees.
- Vultures have powerful beaks that can tear through even the toughest skin.

DESERT BREAKDOWN

Level of Difficulty: 🦈 🦈

While driving across the Kalahari Desert on an archeological dig, your four-wheel drive vehicle breaks down, leaving you stranded. Though you have plenty of water, your radio is not working and you cannot call for help. You decide to begin hiking to the nearest desert outpost 20 miles away. You take your water and you also take:

(A) Your cigarettes and coffee

(B) Your hat and a beer

(C) Your hat and a long-sleeve shirt

(D) An extra pair of shoes and a long-sleeve shirt

(turn page for answer)

ANSWER:
(C) **Your hat and a long-sleeve shirt**

A hat will protect your face from sunburn and keep you cooler. Nights in the desert can be very cold, and a long-sleeve shirt will serve to both keep you warm at night and protect you from sunburn during the day. Coffee and a beer will dehydrate you and should be avoided, and cigarettes will dry your mouth and throat and make you more parched.

EXPERT TIP

When traveling in the desert, always alert friends or embassy or consulate officials of your itinerary and ask them to check on your arrival at specific points.

WHICH IS
YOUR WORST CASE?

Jumping from the roof of a three-story building into a Dumpster

— or —

Leaping to the next rooftop 10 feet away?

Be Aware

- The Dumpster may be filled with hard or sharp materials.
- Most people can't leap distances of more than 10 feet.
- Landing in the Dumpster on your stomach can result in a broken back.
- To leap between roofs, you may have to clear obstacles such as gutters or short walls in addition to the space between buildings.

COCKROACHES

- A roach can hold its breath for more than 30 minutes.

- A roach can live for a week without its head.

- A roach may live four years.

- Roaches are highly attuned to movement in air currents around them.

- Roaches need water and will die after a week without it.

- A roach can go a month without eating.

- Roach blood is white.

- Roaches can breathe through their sides.

- Roaches have been on the earth for hundreds of millions of years.

- A roach can withstand radiation equivalent to that released from a nuclear explosion.

120 BILLION DOLLARS . . . ONE EGG CASE FROM A BLACK

TIGER CONFRONTATION

Level of Difficulty: 🦈🦈

On a sightseeing trip to Chitwan National Park in Nepal, you are warned by authorities that there have been several tiger attacks in the area. Undaunted, you begin a three-day hike into the mountains. On your first day, you notice tiger tracks in the dirt but do not come across any tigers. On the second day, while hiking, you stumble upon a large tigress consuming her prey. She looks up, sees you, and goes back to eating. You freeze, then begin to look for an escape route to get away before the animal changes her mind and attacks. Do you:

(A) Run away as quickly as you can, with your back toward the tigress

(B) Back away slowly, still facing the tigress

(C) Swim across any nearby river or body of water

(D) Run backward

(turn page for answer)

WIDOW CAN HOLD MORE THAN 750 EGGS . . . GAS

(B) **Back away slowly, still facing the tigress**

Tigers (and tigresses) generally attack their prey from the rear, biting the neck. Back away slowly but do not run, or you risk triggering an attack reflex. Unlike most big cats, tigers are excellent swimmers, so do not attempt to escape by entering a body of water (tigers may also lounge near a water source).

EXPERT TIP

In general, tigers will stalk their prey over long distances but will "sneak attack" with a coiled pounce; lions are more likely to chase prey over long distances.

EMISSIONS FROM VOLCANOES CONTRIBUTE TO ACID RAIN . . .

BAR FIGHT

Level of Difficulty: 🦈🦈🦈

While at a bar, you have one too many drinks, briefly lose your balance, and accidentally bump a stranger who is standing behind you, spilling his beer. A moment later you feel someone tapping your shoulder. As you turn around, you see that the stranger, drunk and angry, has his fists up and is about to hit you in the face. You don't want to end the evening in the hospital, but you're also not willing to throw the first punch. Do you:

(A) Lean in close, lessening the force of the blow, if you cannot avoid it altogether

(B) Tilt your head back, hoping his punch won't connect

(C) Quickly hide behind your friends, hoping one of them will protect you

(D) Go into a karate-master pose and hope to scare him off

(turn page for answer)

FIRE ENGINES WERE FIRST USED IN THE 17TH CENTURY . . . THE

ANSWER:

(A) Lean in close, lessening the force of the blow, if you cannot avoid it altogether

If you are unable to avoid a punch to the head, tighten your neck muscles, clench your jaw, and move in close to your attacker. You do not want to take the blow after he has fully extended his arm and his punch is moving at full force. The forehead is the safest place to absorb a blow to the face—avoid taking the punch in the eye or nose, which can cause severe injury, or moving backward, which can cause head whipping and brain injury.

Tighten your neck and jaw. Clench your teeth.
A punch can be absorbed most effectively by the forehead.

Deflect the blow with your arm.

WHICH IS
YOUR WORST CASE?

**Encountering a group
of bear cubs
— or —
Encountering a group
of baby alligators?**

Be Aware
- The mother bear will defend her cubs vigorously.
- Any adult alligator may respond to the distress calls of any youngster.
- Bear cubs may be large enough to kill a human.
- An alligator may drag you into a body of water and drown you.

WHAT'S THE WORST
IT COULD BE?

You are climbing a tall mountain and your fingers feel prickly. Is it:

• gloves that are too tight

• carpal tunnel syndrome

• frostnipped fingers. Frostnip affects only the skin and is an early stage of frostbite. Frostnipped digits may be warmed again under your armpits, in your crotch, or on the stomach or another warm area of a companion.

GREASE FIRE

Level of Difficulty: 🦈 🦈

You're having your first dinner party in your new home, and despite the fact that you've been in the kitchen all day preparing the meal you still have several dishes underway when the doorbell rings to announce the arrival of your first guests. You step away from the stove to open the door, and when you return to the kitchen you discover that the pan full of bacon you left frying on the stove has caught on fire. Do you:

(A) Douse the pan with water

(B) Douse the pan with baking powder

(C) Use a dry chemical fire extinguisher

(D) Cover the pan with a tight-fitting lid

(turn page for answer)

OCCURRED DURING A PACIFIC HURRICANE IN 1933 . . . THE REAR

(D) **Cover the pan with a tight-fitting lid**

The best way to put out a grease fire is to suffocate the flames. Put on an oven mitt, preferably a barbecue mitt that will cover your forearm for added protection, and slide a tight-fitting lid onto the pan, keeping your face and chest as far from the flames as possible. Hold the lid in place until the pan becomes noticeably cooler. Oil and water do not mix—water will cause the burning oil to splatter and spread the fire rather than put out the flames. Attempting to smother the fire with baking powder can cause the flames to flare (though baking soda is a viable option if a tight-fitting lid is unavailable). A dry chemical fire extinguisher is not an effective flame deterrent, and the force of the compressed chemical agent can splatter burning material and spread flames.

WALL IN A HOTEL CLOSET IS USUALLY THE EASIEST WALL TO KICK

TRAIN ROOF ESCAPE

Level of Difficulty: 🦈🦈🦈🦈

You're taking a scenic train trip through the Swiss Alps, ending in the small alpine town of Zermatt, near the Matterhorn. While walking from your train car to the dining car, the doors malfunction and you are trapped outside, between cars. You pound on the door and yell for help, but due to the wind, the loud noise of the train's engines, and good sound insulation, no one hears you. Locked out and freezing, you decide to climb up a ladder and onto the roof of the train, move one car down, and make your way to an unlocked door. Once you get to the roof, do you:

(A) Run as fast as you can forward to the other end of the car to lessen your exposure to the freezing wind

(B) Crouch down, lean into the wind, and move side to side with the motion of the train, following a zigzag pattern to the front of the car

(C) Crawl forward in a straight line

(D) Squirm on your stomach toward the back of the train, keeping as much of your body as possible in contact with the car's roof

(turn page for answer)

THROUGH IN THE EVENT OF FIRE . . . LEAVING IMPALED OBJECTS

ANSWER:

(B) Crouch down, lean into the wind, and move side to side with the motion of the train, following a zigzag pattern to the front of the car

You must sway with the motion of the cars, keeping your knees bent, or you risk being thrown off the train. Do not try to move in a straight line, and do not crawl: There will be nothing to grab on to.

EXPERT TIP

If you see a tunnel approaching, lie flat. There will be a small amount of clearance, but not nearly enough to stand.

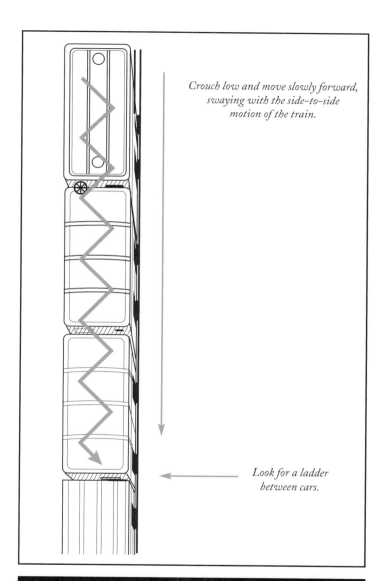

Crouch low and move slowly forward, swaying with the side-to-side motion of the train.

Look for a ladder between cars.

WHAT'S THE WORST
IT COULD BE?

*You are in a restaurant and see a distressed woman
pointing to her mouth and gesturing frantically. Is it:*

• she burned her mouth on too-hot food

• she has accidentally swallowed a fly in her soup

• her airway is obstructed and she needs immediate
  help. Free breathing must be restored within four
  minutes or she may suffer brain damage; if it is not
  restored within eight minutes she will probably
  die. Attempt the Heimlich maneuver by getting
  behind her, placing your arms around her, and
  making quick, sharp upward presses against her
  abdomen with your fist.

FIRE SHELTER

Level of Difficulty: 🦈 🦈

As a volunteer firefighter, you are called to duty in Southern California in October to fight a raging wildfire. Fully equipped, you and your team begin a controlled burn to eliminate scrub and reduce the fuel that is feeding the wildfire. A strong and unexpected gust of wind comes over a ridge and blows embers from your burn in all directions. In seconds, you are surrounded by flames, with little room to run in any direction. Feeling the extreme heat and sensing that you have become trapped, you unpack your emergency fire shelter and begin to deploy it. Do you:

(A) Deploy it on a rocky, open area

(B) Deploy it on the road between two peaks or summits

(C) Deploy it near young, green trees

(D) Deploy it on fresh vegetation

(turn page for answer)

STRUCTION . . . THE STRONGEST KNOWN EARTHQUAKE (9.5

ANSWER:

(A) **Deploy it on a rocky, open area**

A fire shelter protects from heat, not flame, so it must be deployed where there is little chance of flames consuming the area. If possible, deploy the shelter in a rocky, open area or an area where rocks will be between you and the fire. Avoid deploying the shelter on a road between two peaks or summits, or on or near any type of vegetation that can provide fuel for the fire.

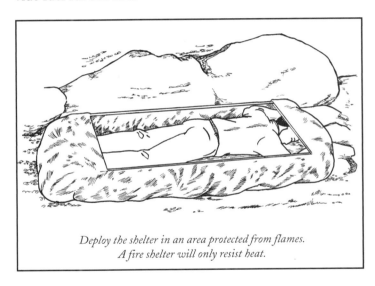

Deploy the shelter in an area protected from flames.
A fire shelter will only resist heat.

WHAT'S WRONG
WITH THIS PICTURE?

(turn page for answer)

CHILE . . . FAST-MOVING WATER ONLY TWO FEET DEEP CAN

ANSWER:

The rider is trying to stop a runaway horse by leaning forward.

Leaning forward is the natural position for a rider who wants the horse to continue running forward. Also, digging your heels into the horse's sides is a sign to the horse that it should run, not stop. Staying in this position is not likely to cause the horse to slow down and may even cause it to run faster.

THE RIGHT WAY

To slow a runaway horse, sit back in the saddle with your feet forward in the stirrups and gently tug and then release the reins. Continue to carefully but firmly tug and release as you say "Whoa!" (Stop!) until the horse begins to slow down and eventually stops. Avoid jerking the reins sharply or pulling them to one side: These actions may cause the horse to stumble and fall, throwing you from the saddle.

Correct.

SWEEP AWAY A CAR . . . A MINE CAN BE DETONATED BY TRIP-

WHICH IS
YOUR WORST CASE?

Being in a car with no brakes
— or —
Being on a runaway train?

Be Aware
- You can't move to a safer crash position before impact in a car.
- You can't steer the train.
- If you pull too hard on the car's hand brake, you can put the vehicle into a spin.
- If you apply the brakes on a train, there is the possibility of derailment.

YOU HAVE COME DOWN WITH SEVERE FOOD POISONING WHILE LOST IN THE WILD. YOU HAVE NO FRESH WATER IN YOUR CANTEEN, AND YOU USED UP THE LAST OF YOUR MATCHES ON YOUR CAMPFIRE LAST NIGHT. YOU MUST FIND WATER TO DRINK OR RISK SEVERE DEHYDRATION FROM THE LOSS OF FLUIDS.

Do you:

DRINK

Sip on unpurified river water—anything is better than dehydration. (The river water might carry even more harmful bacteria, which would make you sicker.)

or

COOK

Get to work making a fire to boil water—more bacteria could kill you. (It will take significant energy to start a fire without matches, and you are already very weak.)

WIRE, DIRECT PRESSURE, TIMER, OR REMOTE SIGNAL . . . THE

EARTHQUAKE

Level of Difficulty: 🦈🦈

You are in San Francisco, riding on a cable car. As the car begins to climb up a steep hill, the earth begins to shake—a sort of shuddering and rolling sensation. The cable car operator immediately stops the car. People run in all directions, some into buildings, others out of buildings. Searching for the safest place to ride out the earthquake, do you:

(A) Run inside the nearest building, unless it is made of bricks

(B) Move into the open, away from power lines, chimneys, and other things that could fall on you

(C) Stand in a doorway

(D) Remain on the trolley

(turn page for answer)

ANSWER:

(B) Move into the open, away from power lines, chimneys, and other things that could fall on you

In an earthquake, if you are outside you should stay there, making sure you are not standing under heavy objects that could fall and injure you (including streetlights). Stay away from buildings, since windows may shatter, sending glass flying, or ornamentation from the building's exterior—or the building itself—may tumble. Be especially aware of power lines that could snap and fall on or near you. Never drive a car, stand under a tree (it could fall), or go inside. Be ready for aftershocks, which can occur hours, days, or even weeks after the initial tremor.

EXPERT TIP

If you are indoors during an earthquake, stay there. Get under a desk or table or move into a doorway or against an inside wall. Stay clear of windows, fireplaces, and heavy furniture or appliances. Stay away from the kitchen.

GRIZZLY BEARS CAN ATTACK HUMANS WITHOUT PROVOCATION

RATTLESNAKE ENCOUNTER

Level of Difficulty: 🦈 🦈

You are horseback riding on a desert ranch when your horse whinnies, then bucks you off its back. You are thrown onto the desert sand, inches from a coiled rattlesnake. Its rattle is vibrating violently, signaling it is about to strike. Do you:

(A) Back away slowly

(B) Grab it just below the head and fling it away

(C) Throw sand in its eyes

(D) Get up and run

(turn page for answer)

ANSWER:

(A) **Back away slowly**

Snakes will bite if startled, and sudden movement may cause them to strike. Move back slowly, keeping in mind that you must be many feet from the snake before you are safe (most snakes can strike a distance of at least half their body length).

When striking, half the snake's body will not leave the ground.

EXPERT TIP

If you are bitten and are unable to get medical treatment within 30 minutes, immediately wrap a bandage tightly two to four inches above the injury site—but not so tight that you restrict blood flow. Do not place ice on the site of the bite; this will make removing the venom more difficult. Do not try to suck out the venom—you do not want it in your mouth, where it might enter the bloodstream.

HAS A FATALITY RATE OF 30 PERCENT . . . PETROLEUM JELLY

WHICH IS YOUR WORST CASE?

Being lost in the wilderness without a compass

— or —

Being lost in the wilderness without water?

Be Aware

- You may wander for days without a compass.
- Without water you may die within three days.
- You can determine direction using the sun, the stars, clouds, or moss.
- Water found in lakes, ponds, and rivers can be safe to drink if boiled.

WHAT'S THE WORST IT COULD BE?

You are in a stadium filled to capacity on the night of the big game and you see a large crowd of people rushing toward you. Is it:

• the home team arriving

• a rush of fans to the beer counter

• angry fans rioting. Stadium stampedes can be fatal to those crushed by the crowd, so do your best to get out of this situation as quickly as possible. Move to the edge of the crowd, near the wall, or go in the same direction as the crowd until you can escape.

COVERED IN LEECHES

Level of Difficulty: 🦈 🦈 🦈

You are canoeing in a lake on a hot summer afternoon, and you jump in the water to cool down. After walking barefoot on the muddy lake bottom and swimming for several minutes, you climb back into your canoe and find several large, black leeches stuck to your legs and feet. What is the best way to remove them without hurting yourself further?

(A) Pour salt on them

(B) Use a fingernail to detach the smaller, anterior sucker, then detach the larger sucker

(C) Grasp the midsection firmly and lift the leech off

(D) Use a lighter to burn the leech off

(turn page for answer)

(B) Use a fingernail to detach the smaller, anterior sucker, then detach the larger sucker

Slide your fingernail across the skin where the smaller oral sucker is attached to dislodge it. The leech's head will move around, seeking to reattach. Once it is free, use the same method to detach the hind sucker, which helps the leech stay in place. The oral sucker may reattach to your finger, but it will not begin to feed immediately. Flick the leech away once it has stopped feeding. Never squeeze, pull, pour salt on, or burn a leech to get it off. It may regurgitate bacteria from its gut into the wound, causing infection.

EXPERT TIP

Leech wounds will heal without treatment
after the anticoagulants lose their effect.

SOAP AND WATER REMOVES MOST RADIOACTIVE PARTICLES . . .

Identify the oral sucker—the small end.

Place your fingernail next to the oral sucker.

Push the leech sideways to break the seal.

Push or pick at the hind sucker
while continuing to flick at the small end.

WHICH IS
YOUR WORST CASE?

Being adrift at sea in a life raft
— or —
Being lost in the Arctic?

Be Aware
- Food is plentiful in the ocean—provided you can catch it—but drinkable water is scarce.
- Snow can be melted for water—if you can heat it.
- In a life raft you are more likely to die of exposure or hypothermia than for any other reason.
- Frostbite can lead to gangrene or infection and can require amputation.

CLIFF HANGER

Level of Difficulty: 🦈

Your eyes are tired from a long, tedious drive through the mountains of the Hindu Kush. You stop your all-terrain vehicle on the side of a steep, narrow track so you can rest your eyes and stretch. Before you climb out, you take your foot off the vehicle's brake but forget to pull up the emergency brake handle. The vehicle creeps backward and partially over the side of the cliff, balancing halfway on and halfway off the road. Do you:

(A) Move quickly to get out as fast as you can

(B) Attempt to drive back onto the road

(C) Move slowly, carefully opening the car door to get out

(D) Kick out the windshield and crawl out over the hood

(turn page for answer)

ANSWER:
(C) **Move slowly, carefully opening the car door to get out**

Avoid any sudden movements that may tip the car and send it over the side. In vehicles with the engine in the front (the vast majority of cars), you will probably have more time to escape if the front of the vehicle (the heavier section) is still on the road. If the front doors are still over land, open one and climb out. Do not attempt to drive the car back onto the road, even if it has four-wheel drive.

EXPERT TIP

When more than one person is in the car, everyone in the front (or everyone in the back) should execute each movement simultaneously to maintain the car's balance. If driver and passengers are in both the front and back seats, the people who are closest to the edge of the cliff should attempt to get out of the car first.

PASSED-OUT PILOT

Level of Difficulty: 🦈🦈

You are flying on a small plane to a remote island when the pilot begins to sweat profusely and gasp for breath. Then he passes out at the controls. Luckily, the autopilot is on, so the plane is not in danger of an imminent crash. However, you realize that you must get on the radio to describe your situation to air traffic control and get further instructions. Which information do you give first?

(A) The plane's call numbers, situation, and destination

(B) The plane's altitude and heading

(C) Your name and flying experience (if any)

(D) The plane's airspeed, fuel situation, and altitude

(turn page for answer)

THAN AT 120 MPH . . . CQD ("COME QUICK DANGER") PREDATES

(A) **The plane's call numbers, situation, and destination**

The critical information air traffic control needs is the identification number of the plane itself (its call numbers are printed on the instrument panel); a description of the situation, including condition of the pilot (is he completely or just temporarily disabled?); and where the plane is going, to determine the fuel situation. After you give this information, you will be asked additional questions and given further instructions. If you get no response on the radio, tune it to 121.5, the emergency channel, and try again.

SOS AS THE INTERNATIONAL DISTRESS SIGNAL . . . BEES SWARM

PLANE CRASHES

- The majority of plane crashes occur during takeoff and landing.

- Pilot error is the number one cause of plane crashes.

- The majority of plane crashes occur in September and December.

- Your chances of being killed in an airplane crash are approximately 1 in 11 million.

- Statistically, the majority of crash survivors were seated in the rear half of the plane.

- Auto accidents kill more people every year than the total number of people killed in air disasters since the dawn of aviation.

- A majority of the public believes travel by automobile is safer then air travel.

- Larger aircraft (more than 30 seats) tend to be safer than smaller planes.

- You have a 2 in 3 chance of dying if your plane is involved in a fatal crash.

- More than 111,000 people have died in plane crashes. Another 78,000 have been injured.

WHEN ESTABLISHING OR MOVING A HIVE . . . RAISE THE HOOD

WHICH IS
YOUR WORST CASE?

Being caught in a blizzard
— or —
Being trapped in a sandstorm?

Be Aware
- Cold weather presents the risk of hypothermia and frostbite.
- Hot weather presents the risk of dehydration and heatstroke.
- You can become lost and disoriented in blowing snow.
- Your cornea can be scratched in a sandstorm, causing loss of vision, infection, or a corneal ulcer.

TIED UP

Level of Difficulty: 🦈

While traveling abroad, you are kidnapped and are being held for ransom. The kidnappers take you to their hideout, hold you against a pole, and pull out some rope to bind your hands. As one of the kidnappers begins to wrap the rope around you, do you:

(A) Take a deep breath, puff out your chest, and flex your wrists against the bonds

(B) Try to distract the kidnapper by talking while he is tying the knots

(C) Make your body go limp

(D) Hide a piece of broken glass in your hand and use it to saw through the bonds

(turn page for answer)

ANSWER:

(A) Take a deep breath, puff out your chest, and flex your wrists against the bonds

By pressing and flexing against the ropes as they are tied, you will gain a few inches of wiggle room once you relax. Using this extra room, you should be able to get your hands free to untie yourself. Going limp will only make it more difficult to escape, and distraction measures are unlikely to work. Never hold a piece of broken glass in your hand: You are more likely to cut your hand than saw through the rope.

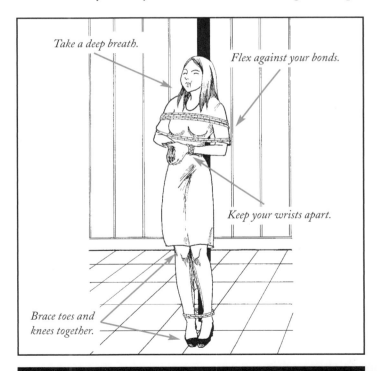

Take a deep breath.

Flex against your bonds.

Keep your wrists apart.

Brace toes and knees together.

OUT THE WINDOW . . . BLOOD IN THE WATER ATTRACTS

WHAT'S THE WORST IT COULD BE?

You hear howling outside your tent. Is it:

• a dog

• an owl

• a gray wolf. Though healthy wolves (especially lone wolves) typically do not attack humans, there have been recorded attacks, and a diseased, starving, or injured wolf can be unpredictable. Leave the animal alone until it wanders away.

YOU ARE LOST IN THE WILDERNESS WITHOUT ANY FOOD, BUT YOU DO HAVE A PACK OF MATCHES. YOUR CELL PHONE AND RADIO ARE NOT FUNCTIONING, AND YOU NEED TO SIGNAL FOR HELP BEFORE YOUR SITUATION GETS EVEN WORSE.

Do you:

TRIANGULATE

Build three small fires in a triangular pattern, an international distress signal. (The fires may be too small to be seen from the air.)

or

CONSOLIDATE

Gather all your available fuel into one location and build a very large bonfire. (One large fire may not be recognized as a distress signal.)

WHAT'S WRONG
WITH THIS PICTURE?

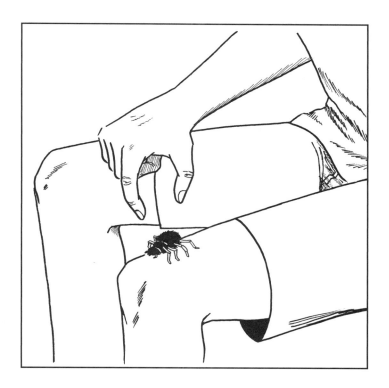

(turn page for answer)

ANSWER:

The man is about to pick up the tarantula with his hand.

Tarantulas may bite, and though most species are not poisonous, a bite may cause severe pain and carries a risk of infection. Also, the sharp bristles on a tarantula's body may cause skin irritation or pose a danger to the eyes.

THE RIGHT WAY

If a tarantula is crawling on you, use a small stick or a rolled-up magazine or newspaper to brush it off. If you cannot dislodge it by this method, stand up slowly and shake your body gently to make it fall off.

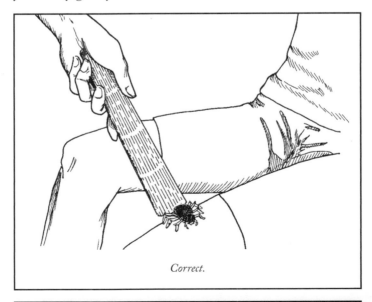

Correct.

SNOWBLIND

Level of Difficulty:

It's late in the afternoon on a bright, sunny winter day, and after several hours of snowmobiling, you and a friend turn around to head back to the lodge. Inching along a ridge above the treeline on your snowmobiles, your friend stops and calls out to you: Everything he sees is red, and his eyes feel like there is sand in them. He is experiencing snow-blindness. You must help him before the sun sets and the two of you are lost in the dark. Do you:

(A) Tell him to listen closely for the sound of your engine and follow by ear

(B) Tell him to stay where he is while you go for help

(C) Blindfold him, put him on your snowmobile, and get him inside as soon as possible

(D) Wait a few seconds for the blindness to pass

(turn page for answer)

TREATING A SEVERED LIMB, TIE OFF ARTERIES WITH FISHING LINE

(C) **Blindfold him, put him on your snowmobile, and get him inside as soon as possible**

Snowblindness results from light overload in the cornea as UV rays are reflected off the bright surface of snowflakes. The injury to the eyes may be serious and permanent. Symptoms include headache, dizziness, seeing red, and extreme sensitivity to light. The best treatment is to immediately get the victim into a dim or dark room until the eyes recover. Wear good-quality sunglasses or goggles with 90 percent UV absorption to combat snowblindness.

EXPERT TIPS

- Put a cool, wet cloth on the forehead—heat makes snowblindness more painful.
- As a preventative measure, reduce glare by blackening under the eyes with charcoal.

OR THREAD . . . SNAILS WITH BRIGHT-COLORED SHELLS MAY BE

WHICH IS
YOUR WORST CASE?

SCUBA diving and running out of air
— or —
Skydiving with a parachute
that fails to open?

Be Aware
- Reserve parachutes must be packed perfectly to deploy correctly.
- Suffocation is a long, slow death.
- Even if you try to save yourself by holding onto a jumping companion, the shock of the chute opening will be severe enough to dislocate your back or break your legs.
- Failing to exhale continuously while surfacing can cause an embolism.

YOU ARE CONFRONTED BY A MUGGER WHO DEMANDS YOUR WALLET, KEYS, AND JEWELRY.

Do you:

COMPLY

Hand over your belongings without argument. (An unsatisfied mugger might harm you anyway.)

or

FIGHT

Attack vital areas of your assailant's body using any weapons available to you. (The mugger could be armed.)

POISONOUS . . . A BITE FROM A BROWN RECLUSE SPIDER CAN

POISON BERRIES

Level of Difficulty: 🦈 🦈 🦈

You take a day hike along a mountain trail and wander off the path for a better view of a spectacular vista. You turn around to get back on the path, but you're unable to find your tracks, and you become lost. You've already eaten the small amount of food you brought along with you, and as dusk approaches you are hungry. You see a stand of bushes with berries and you are tempted to eat a handful to quell your hunger pangs. But before you do, you try to remember the hiker's rhyme about which berries are safe to eat. Is the rhyme:

(A) Berries white, poisonous sight

(B) If berries are red, you'll soon be dead

(C) Berries black, heart attack

(D) Berries blue, that's all for you

(turn page for answer)

CAUSE A SKIN ULCER THAT TAKES MONTHS TO HEAL . . . ONLY 16

(A) **Berries white, poisonous sight**

While there are no hard and fast rules about which wild berries are poisonous, in general terms white berries are more often poisonous than not.

EXPERT TIPS

- Sometimes even handling a poisonous plant to get to berries may cause severe skin irritation.
- Do not assume berries are safe to eat just because you see animals eating them: Birds and rodents may pick apart and eat berries that can be poisonous to humans.
- Cooking poisonous berries does not make them safe to eat.

PERCENT OF AVALANCHE SURVIVORS ARE ABLE TO RESCUE

Plants You Can Eat

black walnuts

burdock

dandelions

mulberries

wild onions

*Hundreds of wild plants are edible, though some require preparation
to make them digestible and/or palatable.*

WHICH IS
YOUR WORST CASE?

Being chased by a herd of elephants
— or —
Being chased by a stampede of bulls?

Be Aware
- Elephants are the largest land animal, weighing 11,000 pounds and standing up to 11 feet tall.
- Bulls are highly attuned to movement and will chase a moving target.
- The force of a single blow from an elephant tusk can kill.
- A bull may charge a person who turns her back to it.

SWARM OF KILLER BEES

Level of Difficulty: 🦈 🦈 🦈

During a visit to El Paso, Texas, you take a hike with your dog Rex. Rex runs ahead of you and begins to jump up and paw at something on a low tree branch. As you get closer, you see that he found a beehive, and the Africanized ("killer") bees he's disturbed are angry and forming a swarm to protect themselves. You start to run away and yell for Rex to follow. You look around and see that there is no shelter nearby. After running 100 yards, to your dismay you see that the bees are still with you, getting ever closer. To escape, do you:

(A) Swat at the bees, hoping to scare them off

(B) Jump into a nearby lake

(C) Run through bushes or high weeds

(D) Lie flat on the ground, face down

(turn page for answer)

(C) Run through bushes or high weeds

If you cannot get indoors, your best chance to escape a swarm of bees is to run through bushes or high grass, which may disrupt their flight. Jumping into a body of water will not do any good; the bees will be waiting for you when you surface. All bees will defend their hive with gusto, but while regular honeybees may follow you for 50 yards, killer bees may chase you three times this distance or more.

If no shelter is available, run through bushes or high weeds.

A SINGLE STORM IS 189 INCHES (15.75 FEET), AT MT. SHASTA,

WHAT'S THE WORST
IT COULD BE?

You are in a high-rise hotel and smell smoke. Is it:

- someone smoking a cigarette in the room next door

- chimney smoke from a fire down the street coming through the open window

- a fire in your hotel. If the door is not hot and the hallway is passable, get to a fire exit. If the door is hot, don't open it. Wedge wet towels under the door to keep smoke out, and stay by the window to wait for rescue.

WHICH IS
YOUR WORST CASE?

Being struck by lightning
— or —
Touching a downed power line?

Be Aware

- Lightning delivers a shock of about 300 kilovolts.
- A downed power line usually delivers between 20 and 63 kilovolts, but contact is more prolonged than a lightning strike.
- Lightning strikes are often fatal, but they can also lead to burns, cardiopulmonary injuries, internal hemorrhaging, or coma.
- You can be shocked without direct contact with a downed power line: Charged particles in the air are also a danger, as are water and other conductive materials on the ground.

STUCK ACCELERATOR

Level of Difficulty: 🦈🦈

It's such a lovely day that you decide to take a scenic drive on a high, winding mountain road. The road climbs higher and higher, and you can look over the edge of a steep cliff that is just to the left of your car, with only a guardrail between you and a steep drop. On a straight patch of road just before a severe hairpin turn, your car shoots forward, seemingly with a mind of its own. The accelerator is stuck, with the pedal touching the floor. You stomp on the brakes, but that only seems to slow you slightly. You stomp on the accelerator to unstick it, but you only move faster. The car continues to pick up speed as you rapidly approach the dangerous curve. Do you:

(A) Immediately open the door and jump out before the car can gain any more speed

(B) Continue to drive the car through the curve in the road, because the turn will slow the car down naturally

(C) Pull the parking brake up gently to slow the car, open the door, and jump

(D) Yank the parking brake with as much force as you can muster to stop the car completely

(turn page for answer)

ARE LESS AGGRESSIVE THAN COMMON WASPS . . . CAPTIVE

ANSWER:
(C) Pull the parking brake up gently to slow the car, open the door, and jump

The parking brake is mechanical and should slow the car down, though it won't stop it. Pull the brake up slowly; do not yank it or you risk causing the speeding car to spin out of control. When the car has slowed sufficiently, open the door and jump, tucking in your head and rolling out and away from the path of the car. Aim for grass or another soft surface. Avoid asphalt, gravel, and trees.

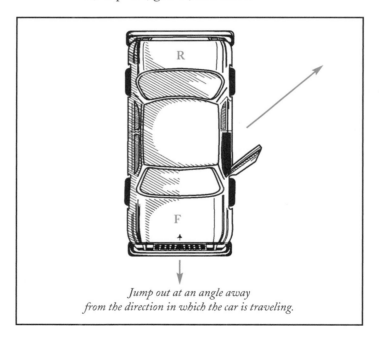

*Jump out at an angle away
from the direction in which the car is traveling.*

WOLVES ARE MORE LIKELY TO ATTACK A HUMAN THAN WOLVES

SINKING CANOE

Level of Difficulty:

On the third day of a white-water canoe trip, your canoe is sitting lower in the river and your feet are wet. The canoe is taking on water. You paddle over to the bank of the river and pull the canoe out of the water. You examine the bottom and find a small hole. What is the best quick fix for the hole?

(A) Fill the hole with a large wad of chewing gum

(B) Patch the hole with duct tape

(C) Patch the hole with your sock

(D) Put all your gear on the opposite side of the canoe to raise the hole out of the water

(turn page for answer)

(B) Patch the hole with duct tape

Duct tape makes an effective patch for small holes and cracks in a canoe. Make sure the surface of the canoe is completely dry before applying the tape. Allow the patch to sit in the sun for an hour for a more permanent fix.

EXPERT TIP

If your canoe has a leaky seam, use a stick to apply pine pitch, the sticky substance found on pine trees, along the leak. Pine pitch is durable and waterproof.

RETIRED; A RETIRED NAME CAN BE USED AFTER 10 YEARS . . . 122

SOMEONE IS CHASING YOU THROUGH THE STREETS WHILE FIRING A GUN.

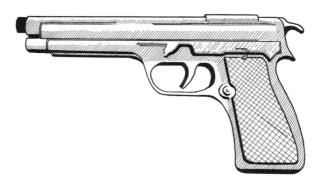

Do you:

RUN IN A STRAIGHT LINE

Sprint for cover, running in a straight line to cover the distance as quickly as possible. (It is easier to hit a target moving in a straight line.)

or

WEAVE

Run in a zigzag pattern to make yourself harder to hit. (Weaving adds considerable distance, causing you to be in the open for a longer period.)

FIRST-CLASS PASSENGERS WERE KILLED ON THE *TITANIC*; 528

WHICH IS
YOUR WORST CASE?

**Being stranded in the wilderness
with a broken arm**

— or —

**Being stranded in the wilderness
with a severe leg wound?**

Be Aware

- Climbing, building a fire, making animal traps, and cooking food may be impossible with a broken arm.
- Moving may be impossible with a severe leg wound.
- Moving a broken arm could damage blood vessels and nerves.
- You can die of blood loss if the femoral artery in your leg is pierced.

FINDING WATER
ON A DESERT ISLAND

Level of Difficulty: 🦈 🦈 🦈

After a terrible storm, your pleasure boat has sunk, leaving you alone on a tiny desert island. Though you have managed to catch several fish to eat, you do not have any water to drink. What is the best way to find drinkable water?

(A) Suck the eyeball areas and spines of fish

(B) Spread out a shirt to collect rain water, should it rain

(C) Drink salt water in small sips

(D) Dig a hole and look for water

(turn page for answer)

ANSWER:

(A) **Suck the eyeball areas and spines of fish**

There is drinkable water in fish spines (except shark spines) and in the eye sockets of fish; break apart the vertebrae and suck the liquid out.

EXPERT TIP

In arid climates, birds often congregate around cracks in rocks that contain fresh water. Additionally, islands that appear to be dry and barren may have wet, mountainous interiors.

IN FRÉJUS, FRANCE, COLLAPSED IN DECEMBER 1959, KILLING 412

WHAT'S WRONG
WITH THIS PICTURE?

(turn page for answer)

. . . WOLF PACKS USUALLY CONSIST OF

ANSWER:

The woman is jumping from a moving train and attempting to land on her feet.

Hitting the ground feet-first after jumping from a speeding train is likely to cause severe injury, including broken legs, heels, and ankles. You also risk flying forward head over heels, potentially resulting in fatal head trauma.

THE RIGHT WAY

To survive a jump from a moving train, wait for the train to slow (as around a bend) and then jump from the train and logroll on the ground until you come to a stop. Keep your arms around your head to protect it. Try to jump into a grassy field or other forgiving surface. Avoid jumping out when the train is in a tunnel.

Correct.

FAMILY MEMBERS . . . NITROGLYCERIN IS EIGHT TIMES MORE

RATS

Level of Difficulty: 🦈🦈

As you stroll down a relatively deserted street late at night, you see an open manhole with a ladder leading down to what you assume will be an underground passageway. You've always been curious about the underworkings of the city, and you wonder where the ladder will take you. You descend the rungs until you are on solid ground. It is dark, so you reach into your pocket for the small flashlight you carry on your key ring. When you turn on the light, you see dozens of rats at your feet. To escape them, do you:

(A) Shine the flashlight into their eyes to scare them away

(B) Stamp your feet

(C) Yell as loudly as you can

(D) Move slowly back to the ladder and climb up

(turn page for answer)

(D) Move slowly back to the ladder and climb up

In general, rats will shy away from human contact. However, a hungry group of rats (a pack may include 60 members) may attack even a large mammal. Rats are also very good swimmers and may swim for a mile or more. To escape from the rats, move slowly back to the ladder and begin climbing up, keeping your eyes on the nearest rat.

A pack of hungry rats may attack even a large mammal.

DESTROYED POMPEII IN 79 C.E. AND SEVERELY DAMAGED NAPLES

WHAT'S THE WORST
IT COULD BE?

You feel a sharp pain in your stomach after eating potato salad. Is it:

• gas

• a cramp from eating too quickly

• severe food poisoning. You may feel symptoms of food poisoning immediately, and they may include severe pain, gastrointestinal distress, cramps, and diarrhea. If you suspect food poisoning, drink plenty of water and seek medical attention right away.

IN 1906 . . . CHESTER GREENWOOD MADE A FORTUNE SELLING

FOOD POISONING

- ✪ Dented cans may be contaminated with botulism if the seal on the can has been affected.

- ✪ Keep hot foods piping hot and cold foods chilled to prevent bacteria growth.

- ✪ Wash hands before handling foods.

- ✪ Do not use the same knife on meat and vegetables unless they will both be cooked.

- ✪ Wash cutting boards with hot, soapy water after each use, or put them in the dishwasher.

- ✪ Hot leftovers should be stored in shallow containers to promote rapid cooling and reduce bacteria growth.

- ✪ Washing meat and poultry before cooking it does not remove bacteria.

- ✪ Do not allow hot foods to cool to room temperature before storing them.

- ✪ Shigellosis, a food-borne illness, may be in the body for seven days before symptoms appear, including diarrhea, fever, abdominal cramps, and vomiting.

- ✪ If you get food poisoning from a restaurant, alert your local health department to help avoid an outbreak.

HIS INVENTION—EARMUFFS—TO SOLDIERS DURING WORLD WAR I

FROSTBITE

Level of Difficulty: ⊰⊱ ⊰⊱ ⊰⊱

On your way to do some ice climbing in the Andes during wintertime, you are overtaken by a sudden, severe snowstorm. In the whiteout, you become disoriented and lose your way. Because of the blizzard, you are unable to start a fire for warmth, so you decide that your best chance for survival is to dig a snow cave to escape the wind and wait out the storm. Freezing, your boots and socks wet from the snow, you huddle in the snow cave for two days and nights before digging your way to the surface. You remove your boots and are shocked to see that the tips of your toes have turned black. You have frostbite. Do you:

(A) Blow on your toes to get the blood flowing

(B) Build a fire, heat some water, then immerse the affected areas in warm water for 10 to 30 minutes

(C) Build a fire, warm your feet directly over the heat for 5 minutes, and drink plenty of liquids

(D) Wiggle your toes to restore circulation

(turn page for answer)

. . . GO FOR THE EYES OR SNOUT OF AN ATTACKING BEAR . . .

(B) Build a fire, heat some water, then immerse the affected areas in warm water for 10 to 30 minutes

Frostbitten toes can safely be rewarmed in warm (not hot) water, but only if the danger of refreezing has passed and medical treatment is nearby. Never rewarm frostbitten skin using direct heat (open flame, hot water bottle), or additional damage to skin may occur. Rewarming will be accompanied by a severe burning sensation at the injury site.

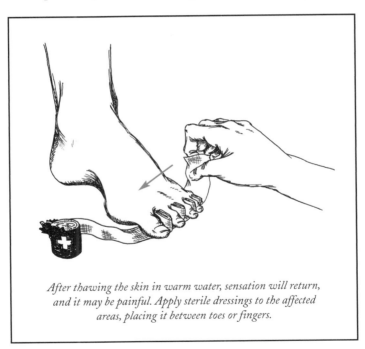

After thawing the skin in warm water, sensation will return, and it may be painful. Apply sterile dressings to the affected areas, placing it between toes or fingers.

HAILSTONES AS HEAVY AS 2.2 POUNDS FELL IN THE GOPALGANJ

BARRACUDA ON BOARD

Level of Difficulty: 🦈🦈

On a deep-sea fishing trip off the Caribbean island of Bequia, you feel a sharp tug on your line, and then it runs out quickly. Fighting what feels like a very big fish, you slowly begin reeling in your catch. After ten minutes, your guide helps you bring in your prize, a five-foot barracuda. Your guide asks if you'd like him to gut, clean, and carve the barracuda into steaks. Do you:

(A) Accept

(B) Accept, but tell him you'll clean the fish yourself once you're back to shore

(C) Accept, but ask just for the flesh near the center of the fish's body

(D) Decline, and throw the fish back into the water

(turn page for answer)

DISTRICT OF BANGLADESH ON APRIL 14, 1986, KILLING 92

ANSWER:

(D) **Decline, and throw the fish back into the water**

Barracuda, which feed near tropical reefs, often harbor dinoflagellate toxins that can cause ciguatera, a type of food poisoning that causes numbness, vomiting, and gastrointestinal distress. In general, you should refuse to eat barracuda to avoid ciguatera; other tropical fish from the same locales (including grouper and snapper) may also harbor the toxins. However, the toxins that cause ciguatera may be highly localized, and a knowledgeable guide may be able to avoid problem areas.

EXPERT TIP

Shellfish can sometimes survive concentrations
of dinoflagellate toxins that would be fatal to humans.

PEOPLE . . . A LARGE MALE RHINO CAN EASILY KNOCK A CAR

CLIFF DIVING

Level of Difficulty: 🦈 🦈 🦈

While hiking in the Grand Canyon, you make camp on the edge of a cliff high above the Colorado River. Before preparing dinner, you take a short nap to regain some strength. You are awakened by a rustling outside your tent. You walk out to investigate and find a mountain lion eying you suspiciously. As it creeps slowly toward you, you back up, getting closer and closer to the edge of the cliff. The cat bends his hind legs to pounce. Trapped, you turn to jump off the cliff and into the river. Do you:

(A) Dive head first

(B) Go straight in feet-first

(C) Curl into a ball

(D) Spread your arms and legs to slow your descent through the air

(turn page for answer)

OVER . . . ERIK WEIHENMAYER BECAME THE FIRST BLIND PERSON

ANSWER:

(B) Go straight in feet-first

When you are unsure of the depth of the water, it is always better to enter feet-first. Keep your feet together and clench your buttocks to avoid internal injuries when you hit the water. As soon as you are submerged, spread your arms and legs wide and move them back and forth to generate resistance and slow your plunge to the bottom.

EXPERT TIP

Hitting the water as described above could save your life, though it may break your legs. If your body is not straight, you can break your back upon entry.

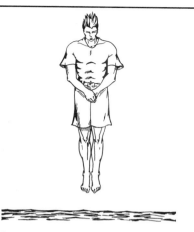

Jump feet–first in a vertical position, squeeze your feet together, clench your backside, and protect your crotch.

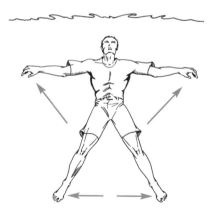

After you enter the water, spread your arms and legs wide and move them back and forth, which will slow your plunge.

CAN TRAVEL AT 450 MPH IN OPEN WATER . . . THE HIGHEST SEA

BULLS ARE RUNNING THROUGH THE STREETS OF PAMPLONA, SPAIN, AND YOU ARE CAUGHT UNAWARES.

Do you:

FLEE

Make for an open door, a fence to jump, or another safe haven. (Bulls can easily outrun humans and are attracted to moving targets.)

or

FREEZE

Stand still and remove an article of clothing—you can use it to distract the bull if necessary. (By standing on the street, you remain vulnerable to a charge.)

CLIFFS IN THE WORLD, AT 3,300 FEET, ARE ON THE NORTH COAST

ALLIGATOR ATTACK

Level of Difficulty: ⬩⬩⬩⬩

You and a friend are enjoying a picnic on the banks of a large pond. The pond is full of wildlife—as you eat your meal, you see frogs, turtles, and large fish moving in the water. Just as you are about to have dessert, you are startled to discover that what you thought was a large turtle sitting in the shallow water 50 feet away is actually an alligator. It climbs out of the pond and up the bank directly toward you. Do you:

(A) Flap your arms and yell to scare it away

(B) Punch the alligator under its bottom jaw

(C) Get on the alligator's back and force its head down

(D) Back away slowly

(turn page for answer)

(C) **Get on the alligator's back and force its head down**

On land, your best hope of survival is to get on the alligator's back and place steady downward pressure on its neck and head. Once in this position, you may be able to clamp its jaws closed with your hands—most of the animal's mouth strength is in closing its jaws, not opening them. If the alligator continues to attack, jab it in the eyes with your fingers.

EXPERT TIP

Feeding alligators may cause them to lose their fear of humans and become more aggressive. Most attacks occur after humans have fed them.

SUNNING THEMSELVES ON ROCKS, SINCE THEY ARE UNABLE TO

WHICH IS
YOUR WORST CASE?

**Finding a centipede
crawling on your leg
— or —
Spotting a yellow jacket wasp
on your arm?**

Be Aware
- Some centipedes have poisonous venom.
- Wasps may be aggressive and quick to sting.
- Centipedes may be 11 inches long.
- Crushing a wasp releases a chemical that signals
  other wasps in the area to attack.

YOU ARE CAUGHT IN A MAJOR SANDSTORM AND MUST PROTECT YOURSELF FROM INJURY.

Do you:

CLIMB

Move to higher ground—sand grains will not bounce high on grass, dirt, or sand, so this will prevent you from getting "burned" by the sand. (Sandstorms can be accompanied by severe thunderstorms, creating a risk of being struck by lightning.)

or

CRAWL

Stay low and take shelter in a ditch to avoid being hit by lightning during the storm. (The lower you are, the more you may be "burned" by the stinging sand.)

REGULATE THEIR BODY TEMPERATURE INTERNALLY . . . AN

BACTERIA IN WATER

Level of Difficulty: 🦈 🦈 🦈

A jungle hike up a 3,000-foot peak in Panama has left you lost and your water supply running dangerously low. You can distill river water by filling a sock with sand and charcoal and letting the water seep through it to clean out impurities, then boiling the water as an additional precaution. What is the least amount of time you can boil the water while still feeling assured that it is safe to drink?

(A) 30 seconds

(B) 1 minute

(C) 4 minutes

(D) 20 minutes

(turn page for answer)

ORANGE-GOLD "SPACE" BLANKET CAN BE USED FOR

Water should always be boiled or chemically treated before drinking. If sufficient fuel is available, boil the water for 10 minutes. However, a general rule is to boil suspect water for one minute, plus one minute for each 1,000 feet above sea level.

EXPERT TIP

Banana or plantain trees may be used as a source of water. Cut down the tree to a one-foot stump and scoop out the center of the stump into a bowl shape. The roots will continually refill the stump with water for about four days.

SIGNALING RESCUE PLANES: THE COLOR IS RARELY FOUND IN

THE DEADLY OCTOPUS

Level of Difficulty: ➤➤➤➤

In search of underwater adventure, you decide to take a two week SCUBA trip to Australia's Great Barrier Reef. Before your first dive, your instructor warns you about several dangerous sea creatures, including sharks, urchins, and the extremely poisonous southern blue-ringed octopus. Mentally filing away the information, you strap on your tank and regulator and begin a half-day dive. An hour into the dive, you see a small, pale-colored octopus wedged into a crevice in the reef. Looking closely, you see no apparent blue rings and prepare to prod the creature gently so it will move and give you a better view. The diving instructor grabs your arms and pulls you away. After surfacing, does he remind you that:

(A) The rings are not visible when the octopus is at rest

(B) All octopi should be considered deadly

(C) The ink from the blue-ringed octopus causes instant death

(D) The blue-ringed octopus does not actually have rings on its body

(turn page for answer)

NATURE AND DRAWS THE EYE . . . THE BAND-AID WAS PATENTED

ANSWER:

(A) The rings are not visible when the octopus is at rest

Though indeed small (less than eight inches long), the blue-ringed octopus is one of the deadliest creatures on earth. Its colorful rings are visible only when the creature is startled or under attack; otherwise, it appears pale or camouflages its body color to match its surroundings.

EXPERT TIP

The blue-ringed octopus is not aggressive and rarely attacks humans except when handled. But the octopus's bite injects a tetrodotoxin, a neuromuscular paralyzing venom that causes instantaneous respiratory failure, paralysis, and blindness, and is often fatal.

WHICH IS
YOUR WORST CASE?

A plane crashing during takeoff
— or —
A head-on train crash?

Be Aware

- The plane's fuel tanks are full and may explode or burn.
- A freight train may be hauling dangerous and/or flammable chemicals.
- Almost a quarter of air fatalities occur during takeoff.
- Two trains colliding can have an impact of several hundred miles per hour.

YOU ARE VISITING A HOSTILE FOREIGN NATION. YOU HAVE HEARD STORIES OF TRAVELERS BEING UNABLE TO LEAVE THE COUNTRY BECAUSE THEIR PASSPORTS WERE STOLEN, AND YOU DON'T WANT THAT TO HAPPEN TO YOU.

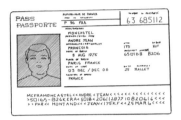

Do you:

CONCEAL

Hide your passport in a secure place on your person and guard it carefully; leave a copy in your hotel safe just in case. (If your passport is stolen or confiscated, you may have difficulty getting back home.)

or

DUPLICATE

Make a copy of your passport and leave the original in the hotel safe or, if you have one, the safe in your room. (The copy might not appease the officials if you are stopped for any reason.)

NEEDED". . . THERE ARE 2,500 SPECIES OF MOSQUITO . . . THE

WHAT'S WRONG
WITH THIS PICTURE?

(turn page for answer)

FIRST INTENTIONAL JUMP FROM AN AIRPLANE WITH A PARA-

ANSWER:

The man is trying to carry the passed-out victim in his arms, risking injury to his back.

Carrying someone in your arms out in front of you requires significant arm and upper body strength and causes severe stress on the arms and lower back. It is also difficult to walk in this position, and you may stumble and fall on top of the person you are trying to help.

THE RIGHT WAY

To walk with a victim who is incapacitated, use a "fireman's carry." Prop the victim up in a sitting position. Leaning into her, place the victim's head and torso over the shoulder of your dominant arm and stand up, holding her legs down in front of you with your dominant arm. By carrying her in this fashion, you will be supporting her with the muscles of your legs and upper back instead of your arms and lower back.

Correct.

CHUTE WAS MADE IN 1919 . . . VENOM CAN CONTINUE TO

TRAPPED IN A LION CAGE

Level of Difficulty: ◂━◂ ◂━◂ ◂━◂ ◂━

On a visit to the zoo, you see an empty lion cage and decide to see what's inside. A few moments after you enter, a lion also enters from his outside play area. The lion looks at you, then begins to wag his tail furiously and paw at the ground. Convinced the lion is about to attack, you turn to leave, but you see that the door has shut behind you. You yell for help, but the lion is advancing toward you. You quickly look around the cage for help. Do you:

(A) Grab one of the steaks that is sitting in a bucket and throw it in the lion's direction

(B) Back away slowly

(C) Pick up a chair and hold it in front of yourself

(D) Try to run past the lion outside into its play area

(turn page for answer)

ENTER THE BODY FOR UP TO TEN MINUTES AFTER A BEE'S

(C) Pick up a chair and hold it in front of yourself

A lion will fiercely defend its food and personal space and may attack if you appear to be charging toward it. Pick up the chair and hold it in front of you in case the lion pounces. A lion will also attack any threat to its cubs, so give them a wide berth. A lion in a zoo may be habituated to the presence of humans and may not attack immediately. However, even zoo lions are wild animals and may act unpredictably. Furthermore, like people, lions have different temperaments, and some are more aggressive than others.

Watch for signs of imminent attack: twitching tail, eye contact, and growling.

STINGER PUNCTURES THE SKIN . . . BLACK BEARS MAY BE BROWN

PACK OF WOLVES

Level of Difficulty: 🦈🦈

A one-week camping excursion in Yellowstone National Park has been an exhilarating, exhausting adventure. Though you've been warned about wolves, you have yet to see one, and your vacation is coming to an end. On the last night of your trip, you hear growling outside your tent. Peeking out, you can see little in the darkness. You reach for your flashlight and walk outside. In the beam of your light, about ten feet away, you see the carcass of a deer on the ground, freshly killed. You hear the growl again, closer this time. Sweeping your light to the left, you see six pairs of eyes watching you. Then you see that the eyes belong to a pack of gray wolves. You freeze. Do you:

(A) Make noise and wave your arms around

(B) Go back inside your tent

(C) Throw sticks and rocks

(D) Run

(turn page for answer)

OR BLONDISH IN COLOR . . . IN 1642, REBELS IN CHINA

ANSWER:

(B) **Go back inside your tent**

Though wolves are meat eaters and generally feed on herbivores larger than themselves, in North America healthy wolves rarely attack humans, even when traveling in packs. Back up slowly, giving the wolves a wide berth, and do not approach pack members or their kill. A wolf may attack if it is sick, extremely hungry, or attacked with stones, but such instances are rare.

EXPERT TIP

Wolves tend to chase their prey into deep snow or onto frozen lakes. If you see wolves around you, move away from these places to solid terrain.

WHICH IS
YOUR WORST CASE?

Riding a runaway horse

— or —

Riding a runaway camel?

Be Aware

- Horses can run or trot for long distances.
- Camels may run wildly and ignore commands.
- Horses are "flight animals," and their first instinct is to run.
- Camels' ears and eyes are specially adapted to cope with sandstorms that may be debilitating to a human rider.

YOUR HIGH-RISE APARTMENT BUILDING IS ON FIRE. YOU NEED TO ESCAPE IN ORDER TO SURVIVE, BUT YOU'RE ON THE 13TH FLOOR.

Do you:

CRAWL

Get down on all fours, since the air will be fresher close to the floor, and quickly crawl down the hallway to the stairs. (The fire may make the hallway impassable.)

or

CLIMB

Make a rope from your bedsheets and escape through the window to another floor. (You may slip and fall to your death.)

TARANTULAS CAN LIVE IN DESERTS, GRASSY PLAINS, SCRUB

AVALANCHE

Level of Difficulty: 🦈 🦈 🦈

During an early spring ski trip to Whistler, British Columbia, you decide to hike "off-piste" into the steep, unpatrolled backcountry to ski the deep powder above the tree line. Just as you are about to begin your long ski run down the mountain, you hear an ominous rumbling. Looking up, you see a huge wall of snow heading down the mountain—an avalanche—and it's coming straight for you. Do you:

(A) Try to stay atop the snow by using a freestyle swimming motion

(B) Quickly dig down into the snow to get under the avalanche

(C) Wait for the snow to hit you, then attempt to ski down on top of it, as if you are surfing a wave

(D) Remove your skis and roll down the mountain like a log

(turn page for answer)

FORESTS, AND RAIN FORESTS . . . MOST NEW CARS HAVE INTE-

(A) Try to stay atop the snow by using a freestyle swimming motion

The snow in an avalanche is heavy and very difficult to dig your way out of. "Swimming" on top of the snow is your best chance to avoid being buried. Avalanches occur in areas where fresh snow has fallen on top of older snow, most often in the afternoons on sunny days, when the morning sun has loosened the snowpack and made it more unstable. Never ski alone, and always carry an avalanche beacon and an avalanche probe.

Try to stay on top of the snow.

RIOR EMERGENCY TRUNK RELEASE HANDLES THAT GLOW IN THE

SINKING CAR

Level of Difficulty: ◄ ◄ ◄

While driving in your car across a causeway, you see that a section of the road just in front of you has collapsed into the water. You do not have enough time to stop your car—you are about to plunge ten feet into the water below. Before the car flies off the roadway and hits the water, you must remember to do one important thing. Do you:

(A) Roll all your windows up

(B) Roll one window down

(C) Unfasten your seatbelt

(D) Turn off your motor

(turn page for answer)

DARK . . . RABIES VICTIMS DO NOT ALWAYS FOAM AT THE MOUTH

(B) **Roll one window down**

As soon as the car sinks into the water, the outside water pressure will prevent you from opening the door. Opening the window serves two purposes. First, it allows you to get out of the car without opening the door. Second, if you cannot get out through the window, it allows water to enter the car and equalize the pressure so you can open the door and escape.

EXPERT TIP

Most cars will sink at a steep angle, because they are heavier in the front, where the engine is. In water deeper than 15 feet, the car may end up on its roof.

Open your window before or immediately after hitting the water. Otherwise, the pressure of the water will make it very difficult to escape.

If you were unable to open a window before hitting the bottom, attempt to break a window with your foot or a heavy object.

WHICH IS
YOUR WORST CASE?

Being locked in a car trunk
— or —
Being tied up?

Be Aware
- In the summer, a car trunk may be over 100°F, and in the winter, it may be freezing.
- Strong, tight bonds may cut off circulation, and such injury could later require amputation.
- In a car trunk, you cannot communicate with your captors.
- If you are tied up, you may also be subject to further torture.

SCORPION STING

Level of Difficulty: ⚔ ⚔ ⚔

You are on a sightseeing trip to Fez, Morocco. You sit down at an outdoor café to have a cool drink and take a break from the hot sun. You remove your sandals and prop your feet up for a few minutes. When you put your sandals back on, you feel a sharp pain in your left foot, then a burning sensation. As you pull the sandal off, a scorpion scurries out and disappears under the building. Should you:

(A) Attempt to capture the scorpion so it can be tested for disease

(B) Attempt to suck out the poison

(C) Rush to a hospital as soon as possible

(D) Put ice on the injury site and monitor symptoms

(turn page for answer)

MAY BE UNABLE TO HEAR RESCUERS FROM INSIDE A SNOW CAVE

ANSWER:

(D) **Put ice on the injury site and monitor symptoms**

Most species of scorpion have venom with low to moderate toxicity and do not present a serious health threat to humans (aside from pain at the injury site). Place ice or a cold pack on the injury site and monitor symptoms carefully. Reactions such as pain in joints, numbness, sweating, and nausea are common. If you experience irregular heartbeat or other life-threatening symptoms, seek medical attention immediately.

Scorpion venom induces anxiety in victims, so it is important to realize that you are not really as anxious as you think you are.

EXPERT TIP

Scorpion venom contains histamines, so an antihistamine is recommended for sensitive people. Scorpions do not leave a stinger in the body. Never attempt to remove venom by sucking at the injury site, since that could spread the venom to the bloodstream of the person sucking.

. . . THE SEAWASP JELLYFISH, FOUND IN THE WATERS OF SOUTH-

THE EYE OF THE STORM

Level of Difficulty: 🦈🦈

A visit to the Caribbean for a week of deep-sea fishing has turned ugly—the weather forecast is calling for a strong hurricane to hit the area. Deciding to stick it out in your rental house, you cover the windows with plywood, turn off the electricity, and listen closely to the radio for storm reports. As rain lashes the building horizontally, a weather reporter announces that the eye has now moved to the southwest of your location. Do you:

(A) Turn the power back on and remove the plywood

(B) Leave all precautions in place and prepare for the worst

(C) Go outside and watch for the winds to shift

(D) Open a window on the side of the house opposite the wind

(turn page for answer)

ANSWER:

(B) Leave all precautions in place and prepare for the worst

The strongest winds of a hurricane are to the northeast of the eye. Keep all precautions in place until the eye has passed and the winds have shifted and calmed sufficiently. Do not uncover or open any windows until the storm has passed and authorities say is it safe to do so.

EXPERT TIP

After the hurricane has passed, do not assume that water-damaged structures or ground are stable. Leave a building immediately if shifting or unusual noises signal a possible collapse.

WHAT'S THE WORST
IT COULD BE?

You hear a muffled scraping sound in your basement.
Is it:

• a mouse

• a squirrel

• a 14-inch Norway rat. Common in areas where
  human population growth is rapid, the Norway rat
  has razor-sharp teeth and claws. One female rat
  can have as many as 84 babies each year.

WHICH IS
YOUR WORST CASE?

A 1-minute bar fight
— or —
A 3-minute round
with a professional boxer?

Be Aware
- An opponent in a bar may be armed.
- A single punch from a professional boxer can be deadly.
- A bar fight can involve more than one opponent.
- Professional boxers are trained to take or dodge blows.

EMPTY SCUBA TANK

Level of Difficulty:

You are SCUBA diving to a shipwreck at a depth of 60 feet. After half an hour of exploration, your equipment malfunctions, and air is no longer coming through your regulator. Do you:

(A) Keep your regulator in your mouth, breathing in and out normally as you surface

(B) Keep your regulator in your mouth, inhale, and hold your breath as you surface

(C) Keep your regulator in your mouth and exhale slowly and continuously as you surface

(D) Remove your regulator and swim to the surface as quickly as possible

(turn page for answer)

ANSWER:

(C) Keep your regulator in your mouth and exhale slowly and continuously as you surface

You must surface slowly—do not rise faster than your air bubbles—and exhale continuously to release the air from your lungs. As you get closer to the surface, the air in your lungs expands, so you do not want to hold your breath completely; do not expel all your air immediately or you will be out of air. As you swim to the surface, keep your airway straight, and keep your regulator in your mouth. If possible, share air with a dive mate as you surface slowly.

Keep your regulator in your mouth.

Keep your airway as straight as possible by looking toward the surface.

Swim at a slow to moderate rate, exhaling continuously.

RECORDED TEMPERATURE WAS 136 DEGREES FAHRENHEIT AT AL

PORTUGUESE
MAN-OF-WAR

Level of Difficulty: ⫘ ⫘ ⫘

While swimming in the warm waters off the coast of Aruba, you notice a violet-colored, balloonlike creature in the water nearby. Moments later, you feel an intense stinging on your leg, and you are overcome with pain. Your leg begins to spasm and you are barely able to get back to the shore. You collapse on the beach and look at your leg—it's covered with extremely painful raised lesions. Two locals notice your plight and immediately know the cause—you have been stung by a Portuguese man-of-war. They offer several remedies for treating the sting. Should you:

(A) Put rubbing alcohol on the wound

(B) Rinse the wound with seawater and treat with ice

(C) Urinate on the wound

(D) Apply vinegar to the wound, then cover it with meat tenderizer

(turn page for answer)

ANSWER:

(B) **Rinse the wound with seawater and treat with ice**

Never, ever touch or rub the affected area with your bare hands: Any remaining nematocysts from the tentacle may release more toxins and cause further injury. Applying alcohol, urine, vinegar, or any other foreign substance may also cause further toxin release and aggravate symptoms. After thoroughly rinsing the wound with seawater, put ice in a plastic bag and place the compress on the injury site to reduce pain and swelling. Once the wound has been cleaned with seawater, a topical sunburn or cortizone cream can be used to treat pain or itching.

EXPERT TIPS

- The Portuguese man-of-war cannot always been seen in the water. Tentacles may break away and inflict stings just as potent as those from attached tentacles. Even dead specimens stranded on the beach can cause stings.
- The Portuguese man-of-war can be found around the world on exposed warm-water ocean beaches after strong onshore winds.

DEHYDRATION

Level of Difficulty: ⬥⬥⬥

On an archeological dig in China's Gobi desert, you and a colleague decide to venture off in your four-by-four to dig in a highly remote area. An hour into your journey, your vehicle breaks down and you have to walk back to camp. With the temperature reaching 120°F, you both quickly become dehydrated. On the verge of passing out, you spot your camp in the middle distance. When you arrive, sunburned and weary, a friend offers you her canteen of water. Knowing your dehydration is severe, do you:

(A) Accept the water, but ask her to mix it with sugar, salt, and baking soda

(B) Accept the water, and ask her to mix it with honey

(C) Refuse the water, and ask for a soft drink

(D) Refuse the water, and ask for a martini

(turn page for answer)

(A) **Accept the water, but ask her to mix it with sugar, salt, and baking soda**

Water alone will not replace the electrolytes lost from dehydration caused by excessive perspiration. Never drink plain water when trying to recover: instead, drink a sports drink, or add one quarter teaspoon of salt, one quarter teaspoon of baking soda, and two tablespoons of sugar to a liter of water.

EXPERT TIP

When you are severely dehydrated, consume a mashed banana, coconut milk, or ripe citrus juice to replace lost potassium in addition to the sugar, salt, and baking soda mixture recommended above.

WHAT'S WRONG
WITH THIS PICTURE?

(turn page for answer)

CAN BE EIGHT INCHES LONG . . . THE TUNGUSKA EVENT, AN AIR

ANSWER:

The woman is trying to climb out of a hole in the ice by leaning backward to push up with her hands and elbows.

Putting the entire weight of your body on a small section of thin ice is likely to cause the ice to break further and will not help you climb out. The ice immediately around the hole is thin (remember, you just fell in) and will crack easily under pressure.

THE RIGHT WAY

Using house keys, nails, or another sharp object, try to gain traction on the surface by reaching as far as you can and then sticking these metal implements into the ice. Once you have a solid grip and are not sliding back into the water, slowly inch forward, one hand after the other, pulling your torso and then your lower body out of the water and onto the ice. Move slowly away from the hole and onto thicker ice, but stay on your belly to distribute your weight evenly.

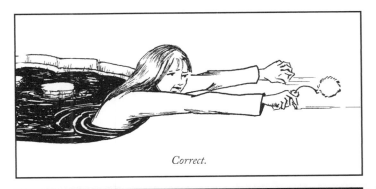

Correct.

EXPLOSION CAUSED BY A METEOR, FELLED 60 MILLION TREES IN

WHICH IS YOUR WORST CASE?

Facing a tiger

— or —

Facing a killer whale?

Be Aware
- Tigers have larger canine teeth than any other carnivorous animal on land.
- Killer whales always hunt in groups.
- Tigers can run as fast as 35 mph for short periods.
- A killer whale swallows its prey whole.

YOU'VE MANAGED TO HIT YOUR GOLF BALL VERY CLOSE TO THE WATER HAZARD. AS YOU APPROACH IT TO ASSESS YOUR COURSE OF ACTION, YOU NOTICE AN ALLIGATOR NEAR YOUR BALL. YOU ESTIMATE THAT THE GATOR IS ABOUT FOUR FEET LONG.

Do you:

CONTINUE TO PLAY

Play your ball as you normally would, ignoring the gator completely. (Alligators may mistake a golf ball for an egg and vigorously defend it as such.)

or

RETREAT

Take a penalty and let the alligator have the ball. (Alligators less than four feet long are not considered deadly to humans.)

SIBERIA IN 1908 . . . THE GABOON VIPER OF TROPICAL AFRICA

VOLCANO

Level of Difficulty: ✦ ✦ ✦

You are exploring Anak Krakatoa, west of Java, the volcano that arose where Krakatoa once stood before its eruption made the entire island of Rakata disappear. Though Anak Krakatoa is a popular tourist destination, the black ash ground is hot, and white steam rises from cracks in the rock. No one is certain of when Anak Krakatoa might blow, but the steam is becoming more intense and the ground is beginning to rumble. You think an eruption is beginning. Should you:

(A) Run as far as you can, as quickly as possible

(B) Take shelter inside the nearest building and lie flat

(C) Take shelter inside the nearest building and move to the highest floor possible

(D) Climb the nearest tree

(turn page for answer)

HAS FANGS 2 INCHES LONG, THE LONGEST OF ANY SNAKE . . .

ANSWER:

(C) Take shelter inside the nearest building and move to the highest floor possible

At the beginning of an eruption, the greatest dangers are from poisonous gases and falling rock. Get indoors and shut all windows, but do not lie flat: Carbon dioxide is denser than air and collects near the ground.

If you are caught amid falling debris, roll into a ball to protect your head.

EXPERT TIP

If time permits, get into a car and evacuate the area, but be aware that lava flows may travel at 200 mph, faster than a car can drive. Since volcanic ash can quickly clog the radiator and engine of your car, avoid driving except to evacuate.

IN THE JUNGLE, SPREAD THE DIRT FROM A TERMITE MOUND ON

RISKY FLIGHT

Level of Difficulty: 🦈 🦈 🦈

You would like to convince a less-adventurous friend who is terrified of flying to join you on a trip to Italy. After doing research on statistics regarding airplane crashes, you present her with the safest possible flight and explain how you've lessened your risks. Which of the following flights will you offer?

(A) Take a nonstop, 6 PM flight from New York to Rome in August

(B) Take a nonstop, 6 PM flight from New York to Rome in October

(C) Take a midday flight from New York to London and then London to Rome

(D) Take an evening flight from New York to Boston, Boston to London, and London to Rome

(turn page for answer)

A majority of plane crashes occur during takeoff and landing cycles, so reducing the number of legs you fly by flying nonstop will slightly lessen your risk of a crash. Many crashes are also caused by inclement weather, so flying during peak thunderstorm times, which are in the late evening in the summer months, should also be avoided. Flying at night is not more or less safe than flying during daylight hours.

EXPERT TIP

When flying, wear long-sleeved shirts and long pants made of natural fibers. Most synthetic materials will melt at a relatively low temperature.

VEHICLE DURING A SANDSTORM, BACK INTO THE WIND TO

WHICH IS
YOUR WORST CASE?

**Attempting to catch fish
without a rod**

— or —

**Attempting to catch wild animals
with a homemade snare trap?**

Be Aware
- It is relatively easy to make a spear or a fishnet.
- Snare traps can be set and left to catch prey at any time.
- Fishing can be time consuming.
- You might need to set 8 to 10 traps at a time to catch just one animal.

WHILE OUT ON A SHORT FISHING TRIP IN YOUR SMALL BOAT, YOU SEE THAT A TSUNAMI IS APPROACHING.

Do you:

RETURN

Make your way back to shore as fast as you can and, once there, get to high ground as quickly as possible. (Tsunamis can cause destruction up to five miles inland.)

or

DEPART

Head into the wave toward open water—tsunamis cause damage in the shallows and are sometimes not even felt in deeper water. (Return waves could drag you miles out to sea.)

REDUCE PITTING OF THE WINDSHIELD . . . COUNT THE DOORS

PORCUPINE CHARGE

Level of Difficulty: 🦈 🦈

A summer hiking trip to Anchorage, Alaska, has been a beautiful, adventure-filled outing. You've gone fishing; spotted bears, caribou, and eagles; and hiked on a glacier. Sitting outside your tent one evening, you spot movement in a nearby bush. Walking over to investigate, you come across a porcupine. The animal sees you, and you both freeze. Observing the creature's needle-like quills standing up straight, you worry that you might be stuck if the porcupine charges. Do you:

(A) Speak to the porcupine in a calming voice

(B) Back away slowly

(C) Walk away at a normal pace

(D) Get behind a tree in case the porcupine throws its quills

(turn page for answer)

ANSWER:

(C) **Walk away at a normal pace**

Porcupines are herbivores and won't attack a human unless severely provoked, but the porcupine's sharp quills are its natural defense against predators and are difficult and painful to remove. Walk away from the porcupine, or continue to observe it until it wanders away from you. Porcupines cannot "throw" their quills, although some quills may become dislodged as the animal shakes its tail.

EXPERT TIP

Before a porcupine will release its quills into a predator, it will clatter its teeth, erect its quills, and simultaneously release a nasty scent. Quills are used only if the threat has not been deterred by these other means.

HELP YOU ESCAPE SHOULD SMOKE FILL THE HALLWAY . . . A

HOTEL FIRE

Level of Difficulty: 🦈 🦈 🦈 🦈

You are staying in a room on the fourth floor of a high-rise hotel, and the fire alarm goes off. You smell smoke, but you can't see it, and it's not overpowering. You place the back of your hand on the metal handle of the door to the hallway to test whether it's safe for you to evacuate the hotel, and the handle is warm to the touch. Do you:

(A) Tie two bedsheets together to make a rope, then climb down

(B) Soak a sheet in water, hang it from the top of the window, then open the window and get in your "tent" to breathe outside air

(C) Climb onto the window ledge and jump into the swimming pool directly below your room

(D) Climb onto the window ledge to wait for the fire department

(turn page for answer)

SERIES OF AVALANCHES OCCURRED IN THE SWISS, AUSTRIAN,

(B) Soak a sheet in water, hang it from the top of the window, then open the window and get in your "tent" to breathe outside air

Two sheets tied together will give you only about 12 feet of rope, or only enough to climb down one story. If you cannot get to the hallway and a fire exit, make a survival "tent" using the wet sheet to offer some protection from heated air and smoke particles. With the window open, breathe the cool outside air while you signal to firefighters. Do not jump from any window higher than two stories, and do not try to walk on a window ledge—you may fall before the fire department is able to rescue you.

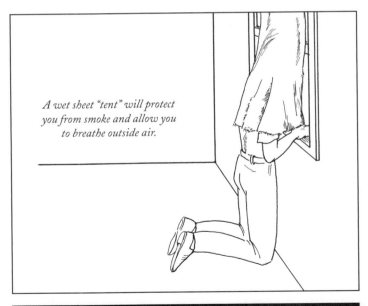

A wet sheet "tent" will protect you from smoke and allow you to breathe outside air.

AND ITALIAN ALPS ON JANUARY 20, 1951, KILLING 240 AND

JUNGLE SURVIVAL

☼ Insect bites and infection of bite sites are the primary danger in the jungle.

☼ Most jungle settlements are on the banks of rivers.

☼ The jungle canopy may occlude the sun and make hiking and navigation difficult.

☼ Alligators, crocodiles, and caimans generally hunt at night.

☼ Do not touch brightly colored amphibians: Their skin may secrete toxic chemicals.

☼ Fruits that are eaten by birds and monkeys are usually safe for humans to eat.

☼ Peel or skin all fruits before eating them.

☼ Wear long sleeves and pants to protect arms and legs from poisonous vegetation, even when the temperature is hot.

☼ Sleep under mosquito netting, and carry anti-malarial pills.

☼ Assume all snakes are poisonous.

TRAPPING 45,000 PEOPLE . . . LAND LEECHES OFTEN HANG FROM

WHICH IS
YOUR WORST CASE?

Being bitten by red fire ants
— or —
Being stung by a scorpion?

Be Aware
- Venom from fire ants can cause nausea, dizziness, and vomiting.
- A sting from a scorpion can cause severe pain in joints and induce panic.
- Fire ant bites may show up days after you are attacked.
- Scorpion venom may cause anaphylactic shock.

SWIMMING THROUGH PIRANHAS

Level of Difficulty: 🦈🦈🦈

You are on a boat trip down the Amazon. Two days into the trip, the boat develops engine trouble and begins to drift uncontrollably down the river. With a waterfall approaching, the captain tells the passengers the best chance for survival is to jump off the boat and swim or wade to the riverbank. You anxiously look over the side of the boat and see a school of piranhas. You must jump. Do you:

(A) Throw a large object into the center of the school to disperse the fish

(B) Drop some raw meat over one side of the boat and lower yourself into the water on the opposite side

(C) Remove your clothes and throw them overboard ahead of yourself, then swim quickly to shore

(D) Cover all bare skin with oil, then quickly swim ashore

(turn page for answer)

TREES AND FEED ON MAMMAL BLOOD . . . MOST PASSENGER

(B) **Drop some raw meat over one side of the boat and lower yourself into the water on the opposite side**

Piranhas are drawn to blood and flesh, so dropping meat over the side should distract them enough for you to get away. However, the fish may go into a feeding frenzy and bite and snap at anything while they feed, so jump on the other side of the boat.

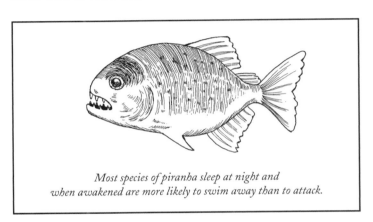

Most species of piranha sleep at night and when awakened are more likely to swim away than to attack.

EXPERT TIP

In piranha country, avoid approaching docks and piers where fish are cleaned; the blood and offal will attract the fish.

TRAIN CARS DO NOT HAVE LADDERS ON THE SIDES . . . AS A

WHAT'S WRONG
WITH THIS PICTURE?

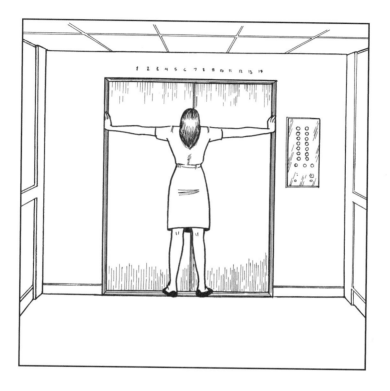

(turn page for answer)

FRESHLY KILLED ANIMAL'S BODY COOLS, TICKS AND OTHER PARA-

The person is bracing herself in the doorway of a falling elevator.

Bracing yourself in the doorway of a falling elevator is unlikely to increase your chances of surviving the accident. The elevator cabin may compact on impact, making your effort relatively pointless as a protective measure. Further, do not jump to save yourself—the elevator's downward velocity will make timing such a jump virtually impossible, and you will have no way of knowing when the cabin is about to hit the bottom of the hoist way.

THE RIGHT WAY

Lie flat on your stomach and spread your legs to evenly distribute your weight on the floor of the elevator. As the cabin hits the bottom of the hoist way, the ceiling is likely to cave in. Cover your head with your arms to protect it from falling lights, paneling, and steel parts.

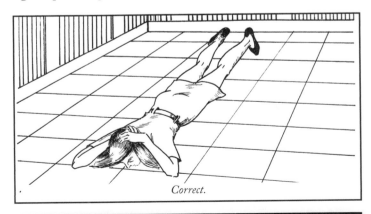

Correct.

SITES FALL OFF . . . THE FASTEST RECORDED SURFACE WIND

CRASHING THROUGH ICE

Level of Difficulty:

On a trip to Sjusjoen, Norway, you rent a cabin on the shore of a frozen lake to do some ice fishing. The lake appears to be frozen solid, but you notice some cracks that alarm you. You ask a local whether the lake is safe to drive on, and he assures you that it's fine. Still wary, you want to know the thickness of the ice before you drive out onto the lake. What is the minimum thickness the ice must be in order to safely support your car?

(A) 6 inches

(B) 8 inches

(C) 10 inches

(D) 12 inches

(turn page for answer)

ANSWER:
(B) **8 inches**

Cars need at least 8 inches of clear, solid ice to safely travel on a frozen lake. Be on the lookout for snow on the ice surface; the weight of the snow can reduce the bearing capacity of the ice and may insulate it, slowing the freezing process.

EXPERT TIPS

When driving a car on ice:
- Drive across any cracks at a right angle.
- Do not leave a car parked in the same place on the ice for long periods.
- Do not drive several vehicles close together on the ice surface.
- Carry several long nails and a length of rope. These can be useful if you fall through the ice and need to climb back out.

FRIGID WATER
SURVIVAL TECHNIQUE

Level of Difficulty: 🦈 🦈 🦈

You are on a fishing boat in the cold waters of the North Atlantic when a huge storm whips up and rocks you and your boat for hours. You put on a life jacket. The boat springs a leak and capsizes, and you are left floating in the frigid water, unable to locate any fellow crew members or floating debris. What position is best for conserving heat so you can survive until you are rescued?

(A) Place your hands on top of your head, keeping your arms above the icy water

(B) Float on your stomach with your legs crossed at the ankles

(C) Float on your back with your arms crossed on your chest

(D) Cross your ankles and bring your knees up, using your arms to pull them to your chest

(turn page for answer)

ANSWER:

(D) Cross your ankles and bring your knees up, using your arms to pull them to your chest

Keep your hands high on your chest or neck to keep them warm, and do not remove clothing; this position can reduce heat loss by 50 percent.

EXPERT TIP

Cold water saps body heat 25 times faster than air of the same temperature, and water colder than 70°F can cause hypothermia.

WHICH IS
YOUR WORST CASE?

Eating raw deer meat
— or —
Drinking polluted water?

Be Aware
- You can contract tuberculosis, M. bovis, simply by handling raw deer meat.
- The water may cause severe diarrhea or dysentery.
- Raw deer meat may carry the deadly hepatitis E virus.
- If you boil the water, you will destroy bacteria but not chemical pollutants.

A RIOT BREAKS OUT DURING YOUR VISIT TO A FOREIGN CITY, AND A MOB IS IN THE STREET.

Do you:

DRIVE

If you have a car, try to take it along back roads to the embassy. (You may be pulled from your car and beaten.)

or

WALK

Dress to blend in and try to get to the embassy on foot. (You may be more vulnerable to attack walking out in the open.)

RIP CURRENT

Level of Difficulty:

On a vacation to Manly Beach, near Sydney, Australia, you go for a swim even though a sign indicates a severe danger of rip currents. The water is so inviting that you just can't resist. Forty feet from the sand, the shore begins to recede quickly, and you find you are being pulled out to sea. You are caught in the rip current. To escape the current, do you:

(A) Fight the current and swim straight to shore

(B) Swim 20 yards farther out, until you feel the rip current subside

(C) Swim parallel to shore until you escape the rip current, then head back to land

(D) Dive under water to get below the rip current, then swim to shore

(turn page for answer)

FEET PER SECOND . . . RAMMING A GATE CAN CAUSE A CAR'S

ANSWER:

(C) **Swim parallel to shore until you escape the rip current, then head back to land**

Rip currents are generally 50 to 100 yards long, but less than 100 feet across. Your best chance of escape is to swim parallel to shore until you are free of the water's pull. Never attempt to swim directly to shore in a rip current; you will quickly tire and will not be able to fight the power of the current.

(Direction of rip current)

To escape a rip current, swim parallel to shore until you are beyond its pull.

EXPERT TIP

You may be able to spot a rip current from shore. Look for a long line of sandy or muddy water and debris heading out to sea, perpendicular to shore.

AIRBAGS TO DEPLOY . . . WATER IN CAVES MAY BE HIGH IN DAN-

WHICH IS
YOUR WORST CASE?

Taking a punch in the forehead
— or —
Taking a punch in the solar plexus?

Be Aware
- A hard blow to the head can cause brain damage.
- A hard blow to the gut can damage internal organs.
- A blow to the forehead can cause a concussion or unconsciousness.
- A blow to the solar plexus temporarily paralyzes the diaphragm, which can lead to a seizure.

WHAT'S THE WORST
IT COULD BE?

You are riding on a train and see the engineer running past you toward the back of the train. Is it:

• another passenger is sick

• a toilet is overflowing

• the train is about to collide with something. In a crash, the safest place to be is as far from the front of the train as possible. Move to the last car, if possible, and brace yourself against a forward wall (one at the leading end of the car). If time permits, place pillows and blankets around your head.

WHAT'S WRONG
WITH THIS PICTURE?

(turn page for answer)

KRAKATOA IN 1883 CREATED A TSUNAMI THAT KILLED MORE

ANSWER:

The person is cowering to discourage a mountain lion attack.

Making yourself appear smaller in front of a mountain lion will make you more of a target, since the mountain lion is more likely to attack if it feels it has a size advantage over its prey.

THE RIGHT WAY

To deter an attack, open your arms and coat wide to make yourself appear larger. Pick up small children and hold them high off the ground. Back away slowly, but do not run. If you see a mountain lion crouching and preparing to pounce, throwing stones at it may deter an attack. If the animal does attack, protect your neck at all costs, and use hands and fingers to attack the mountain lion's eyes.

Correct.

OUT-OF-CONTROL CAMEL

Level of Difficulty: ━━ ━━ ━━

You have finally realized your life's dream of visiting Egypt, and while riding on a camel to visit the tomb of Amun Dudu a sandstorm appears on the horizon. Seeing the approaching storm, your camel freaks, taking off deep into the desert. You pull back on the reins and yell "Hut! Hut!" but the camel does not stop. Do you:

(A) Attempt to jump off, knowing that you have no idea how to get back

(B) Hang on tight and pull the reins to one side

(C) Continue to pull back on the reins until the camel becomes so annoyed that it throws you off

(D) Hang on until the sandstorm is upon you—the camel will immediately change directions and take you back to where you came from

(turn page for answer)

LIKELY TO STING . . . AFRICAN-AMERICAN INVENTOR GARRETT A.

ANSWER:

(B) Hang on tight and pull the reins to one side

This will force the camel to run in a circle, and eventually the camel will tire out and simply sit down. If the camel resists and attempts to go in the opposite direction, let it—pull the reins and run the camel in a circle in whatever direction it wishes to go. Camels tire easily and will not generally run very far.

EXPERT TIP

Don't ever head into a sandstorm, which can very quickly suffocate you or "burn" you with swirling sands. If you are caught in one, quickly wet a bandanna and place it over your nose and mouth to avoid sand inhalation. A small amount of lubricant inside your nostrils will also help avoid the drying of your mucous membranes during such a storm.

MORGAN CREATED THE GAS MASK AND THE TRAFFIC SIGNAL . . .

AN AVALANCHE CAUSED BY THE COLLAPSE OF A 500-FOOT SEC-

WHAT'S THE WORST IT COULD BE?

You are in a plane on your way from Los Angeles to Honolulu and you are told mid-flight to put your seat back fully upright. Is it:

• the meal is being served

• the person behind you wants more leg room

• the plane is about to make an emergency landing because of an engine malfunction. After putting your seat back upright, tighten your seatbelt, note the location of the nearest exit, and hold a pillow over your head with your arms. Many people survive a crash only to be injured or killed by post-impact fire and its byproducts (smoke and toxic gases), so be prepared to abandon your belongings and evacuate the plane as quickly as possible after the crash.

WRAPPED BY A BOA CONSTRICTOR

Level of Difficulty: 🦈 🦈 🦈

During a jungle excursion in Colombia, you make camp under several large trees. Exhausted from a long day of hiking, you lie down to rest without fully zipping the door to the tent. You fall asleep. You awaken to the feeling of slight pressure on your legs—you open your eyes to find an eight-foot boa constrictor wrapping its coils around your body. The snake is tightening its grasp. Do you:

(A) Stay relatively still, grab the head, and begin unwrapping the coils

(B) Thrash violently to loosen the snake's grip

(C) Roll on the ground to loosen the snake's grip

(D) Bite the snake (if your head can reach)

(turn page for answer)

ANSWER:

(A) Stay relatively still, grab the head, and begin unwrapping the coils

Struggling against the boa constrictor will only cause it to tighten its grip. However, do not stay completely still, since boas may continue constricting even after they think their prey is dead. Instead, move carefully and begin unwinding the coils from whichever end is closest, while at the same time holding the snake's head with one hand. Boas are not poisonous, and a bite will not kill you.

NING STORM . . . THE ANTARCTIC ICE SHEET IS ALMOST TWICE

KILLER WHALES

- ✪ Killer whales (orcas) are highly social: They travel and hunt in groups called "pods."

- ✪ Orcas are sometimes called "sea wolves" because of their social behavior.

- ✪ The average adult orca is 23 feet long.

- ✪ An orca may beach itself to scare seals or penguins into the water, where pod members will attack them.

- ✪ Orcas hunt animals as small as fish and as large as other whales.

- ✪ Orcas live in all of the world's oceans.

- ✪ An average orca tooth is 3 inches long and curved backward to help shred prey.

- ✪ An adult orca may eat 500 pounds of food each day.

- ✪ Orcas do not chew their food.

- ✪ An orca may swim as fast as 30 mph.

THE SIZE OF THE UNITED STATES . . . THE ONLY PREVENTION OF

WHICH IS
YOUR WORST CASE?

Being buried in an avalanche
— or —
Being lost in a cave?

Be Aware
- Most avalanche survivors do not escape without help from a rescuer.
- A cave will be pitch black, and cave systems can extend for miles.
- You may suffocate under deep snow.
- Caves may contain predators such as wolves, bobcats, or bears.

TONGUE STUCK TO POLE

Level of Difficulty: ◄━

On an especially cold winter's day, you and a friend decide to take a walk. A storm the previous night has left the streets covered in snow, and the temperature is hovering in the low teens. On a whim, you challenge your friend to touch his tongue to a frozen lamppost. He accepts, and seconds later he finds his tongue stuck to the pole. Screaming in pain, unable to pull his tongue off, he pleads for your help. Do you:

(A) Yank his tongue off using one quick tug

(B) Slowly peel his tongue from the pole

(C) Call the fire department

(D) Pour hot water on the tongue and pole

(turn page for answer)

ANSWER:
(D) **Pour hot water on the tongue and pole**

A tongue sticks to a frozen pole when the temperature is cold enough to freeze to the top layer of cells on the tongue when they come in contact with metal. Pulling or yanking the tongue off will cause extreme pain and may leave a wound on the tip of the tongue. Use hot water to warm the lamppost, melt the frozen cells, and allow the tongue to be pulled off easily.

Warming the pole with your hands may also help free a stuck tongue.

CHIGGER INFESTATION

Level of Difficulty: 🦈 🦈

After a full-day hike in Topanga Canyon in Southern California, you return home and notice a persistent itch around your ankles. You take off your shoes and socks and find small red welts and swelling on your feet, symptoms of chiggers. The itching is unbearable, and you need to do something to comfort yourself. Do you:

(A) Go swimming, fully clothed, in a chlorinated swimming pool

(B) Rub nail polish remover on your feet and place your clothes in a sealed garbage bag

(C) Take a hot shower and wash your clothes in hot water

(D) Place your clothes in a 200°F oven and soak in a tub with Epsom salts

(turn page for answer)

ANSWER:

(C) **Take a hot shower and wash your clothes in hot water**

Chigger larvae can be eliminated from the body by showering in hot water and rubbing the affected area with soap and water repeatedly. Clothes should be washed in hot (125°F) water before they are worn again. Immersion in cold water will not kill chigger larvae. Chigger bites may itch even after the larvae have been eliminated. Persistent itching can be treated with hydrocortisone, benzocaine, or calamine lotion.

EXPERT TIP

Chiggers in Asia and the Pacific region
may carry scrub typhus.

QUAKES OFTEN PRECEDE VOLCANIC ERUPTIONS . . . THE GIANT

WHICH IS
YOUR WORST CASE?

Being bitten by a snake
— or —
Being stung by a scorpion?

Be Aware
- Not all snakes are poisonous.
- Scorpions cannot usually deliver enough venom to kill a healthy adult.
- Poisonous snakes inject more venom than scorpions.
- Some scorpions contain powerful neurotoxins, which, ounce for ounce, are more toxic to humans than the venom of cobras.

SURVIVAL
APTITUDE TEST

The Worst-Case Scenario Survival Aptitude Test (WCS SAT) has been developed by the authors and researchers at the Worst-Case Scenario Survival Institute to test crucial survival knowledge and resourceful quick thinking. Mark your answers to the following questions on the score sheet (or a photocopy) on pages 253–254. When finished, consult the table on page 275 to determine your level of survival aptitude and preparedness.

Good luck!

1. ○ ○ ○ ○
   A B C D

2. ○ ○ ○ ○
   A B C D

3. ○ ○ ○ ○
   A B C D

4. ○ ○ ○ ○
   A B C D

5. ○ ○ ○ ○
   A B C D

6. ○ ○ ○ ○
   A B C D

7. ○ ○ ○ ○
   A B C D

8. ○ ○ ○ ○
   A B C D

9. ○ ○ ○ ○
   A B C D

10. ○ ○ ○ ○
    A B C D

11. ○ ○ ○ ○
    A B C D

12. ○ ○ ○ ○
    A B C D

13. ○ ○ ○ ○
    A B C D

14. ○ ○ ○ ○
    A B C D

15. ○ ○ ○ ○
    A B C D

16. ○ ○ ○ ○
    A B C D

17. ○ ○ ○ ○
    A B C D

18. ○ ○ ○ ○
    A B C D

19. ○ ○ ○ ○
    A B C D

20. ○ ○ ○ ○
    A B C D

21. ○ ○ ○ ○
    A B C D

22. ○ ○ ○ ○
    A B C D

23. ○ ○ ○ ○
    A B C D

24. ○ ○ ○ ○
    A B C D

25. ○ ○ ○ ○
    A B C D

26. ○ ○ ○ ○
    A B C D

27. ○ ○ ○ ○
    A B C D

28. ○ ○ ○ ○
    A B C D

29. ○ ○ ○ ○
    A B C D

30. ○ ○ ○ ○
    A B C D

31. ○ ○ ○ ○
    A B C D

32. ○ ○ ○ ○
    A B C D

33. ○ ○ ○ ○
    A B C D

(continued on next page)

34. ○ ○ ○ ○
    A B C D

35. ○ ○ ○ ○
    A B C D

36. ○ ○ ○ ○
    A B C D

37. ○ ○ ○ ○
    A B C D

38. ○ ○ ○ ○
    A B C D

39. ○ ○ ○ ○
    A B C D

40. ○ ○ ○ ○
    A B C D

41. ○ ○ ○ ○
    A B C D

42. ○ ○ ○ ○
    A B C D

43. ○ ○ ○ ○
    A B C D

44. ○ ○ ○ ○
    A B C D

45. ○ ○ ○ ○
    A B C D

46. ○ ○ ○ ○
    A B C D

47. ○ ○ ○ ○
    A B C D

48. ○ ○ ○ ○
    A B C D

49. ○ ○ ○ ○
    A B C D

50. ○ ○ ○ ○
    A B C D

THE WORST-CASE SCENARIO SURVIVAL APTITUDE TEST

ANALOGIES

1 Keys are to escaping from a frozen lake as stout pole is to:
(A) Swimming out of a river
(B) Floating on quicksand
(C) Walking on snow
(D) Hiking in the forest

2 Shark is to blood as bear is to:
(A) Garbage
(B) Water
(C) Tree
(D) Grass

3 Water is to desert as warm clothing is to:
(A) Body
(B) Mountains
(C) Winter
(D) City

4 Tornado is to basement as tsunami is to:
(A) Tall building
(B) Landslide
(C) Swimming
(D) Running

INVERTEBRATE . . . IGUAÇU FALLS, ON THE BORDER OF

5 Lyme disease is to tick as rabies is to:

(A) Bee

(B) Scorpion

(C) Raccoon

(D) Fire ant

6 Swimming at low tide is to sharks as swimming at dawn is to:

(A) Piranhas

(B) Leeches

(C) Crocodiles

(D) Alligators

7 Eyes and nose are to alligator as eyes and gills are to:

(A) Piranha

(B) Shark

(C) Barracuda

(D) Crab

8 Rolling like a log is to jumping from a moving train as rolling in a somersault is to:

(A) Escaping from an airplane crash

(B) Escaping from a sinking car

(C) Jumping from a car with no brakes

(D) Leaping into a river

9 Coat hanger is to locked car door as kicking is to:
  (A) Locked house door
  (B) Lost shoe
  (C) Broken leg
  (D) Quicksand

10 Fingernail is to leech as tweezers are to:
  (A) Mosquito
  (B) Tick
  (C) Scorpion
  (D) Mountain lion

11 Crawling is to volcanic eruption as struggling is to:
  (A) Quicksand
  (B) Mountain lion
  (C) Shark
  (D) Alligator

12 Warm water is to frostbite as direct pressure is to:
  (A) Head wound
  (B) Bee sting
  (C) Spider bite
  (D) Broken bone

FEET . . . PRINCE CHARLES OF ENGLAND NARROWLY ESCAPED

13 Sharing a parachute is to skydiving as sharing a regulator is to:

(A) Falling elevator
(B) SCUBA diving
(C) Surfing
(D) Swimming

14 Wet towels are to hotel fire as bandanna is to:

(A) Sandstorm
(B) Snowstorm
(C) Sweaty brow
(D) Dog bite

15 Radio is to plane out of control as fire is to:

(A) SCUBA diving
(B) Volcanic eruption
(C) Lightning strike
(D) Lost in the wilderness

16 Lying flat is to plummeting elevator as standing tall is to:

(A) Bear
(B) Tick
(C) Mountain lion
(D) Python

17 Spear is to fish as snare is to:
(A) Rodent
(B) Mugger
(C) Lobster
(D) Bat

18 Eyes are to bird attack as neck is to:
(A) Rattlesnake bite
(B) Mountain lion attack
(C) Shark attack
(D) Killer bee sting

FILL-IN-THE-BLANK

19 Sandbars often trap _____ at low tide.
(A) Sharks
(B) Leeches
(C) Crabs
(D) Piranhas

20 _____ is a good thing to offer a corrupt border official.
(A) Gourmet food
(B) Pocket change
(C) Liquor
(D) Used clothing

21 Avoid swimming in the ocean with _____.

(A) Shiny jewelry

(B) A red bathing suit

(C) A green bathing suit

(D) A dog

22 Mountain streams are never home to _____.

(A) Frogs

(B) Piranhas

(C) Leeches

(D) Bacteria

23 A defibrillator is used to treat failure of the _____.

(A) Liver

(B) Lungs

(C) Kidneys

(D) Heart

24 During a thunderstorm, it is best to avoid _____.

(A) Getting wet

(B) Standing under a lone tree

(C) Standing near a window

(D) Lying in an open field

MOST POWERFUL BIRDS IN THE WORLD . . . WHEN LOST IN THE

25 A snake will generally strike from a _____ position.
(A) Relaxed
(B) Completely straight
(C) Coiled
(D) Balled

26 "CPR" stands for _____.
(A) Cardiopulmonary Resurrection
(B) Cardiopulmonary Reactivation
(C) Cardiopulmonary Resuscitation
(D) Cardiopulmonary Revitalization

27 The true meaning of "tsunami" is _____.
(A) Tidal wave
(B) Harbor wave
(C) Super wave
(D) Microwave

28 A "Quin-Zhee" is also known as a _____.
(A) Quonset hut
(B) Mountain lion
(C) Snow shelter
(D) Lean-to

DESERT, TRAVEL ON RIDGES, NOT IN VALLEYS, AND OCCASION-

29 A "yoke" on an airplane is the _____.

(A) Throttle

(B) Steering wheel

(C) Altitude indicator

(D) Breakfast option

30 "Ion mobility spectroscopy" is used to _____.

(A) Measure the heart rate

(B) Detect radiation levels

(C) Detect explosives

(D) Find buried treasure

31 Your "obliques" can be found in your _____.

(A) Feet

(B) Abdomen

(C) Arms

(B) Thighs

32 *Carcharodon carcharias* is also known as a

_____.

(A) White shark

(B) Brown shark

(C) Grizzly bear

(D) Black bear

33 Ducques (pronounced "ducks") are _____.
- (A) Blazes on trees
- (B) Piles of rocks
- (C) Mounds of earth
- (D) French ducks

34 "Saltation" is a word that describes_____.
- (A) The bouncing movement of small particles, like grains of sand
- (B) The curing of meats using salt
- (C) The act of adding salt to food
- (D) The act of saluting

35 A "riptide" is more accurately called a _____.
- (A) Tidal squeeze
- (B) Rip wave
- (C) Dead man's tide
- (D) Rip current

36 "Hirudiniasis" occurs when _____.
- (A) A scorpion injects venom
- (B) A severed limb begins to rot
- (C) A leech invades a body orifice
- (D) A bee stings the eyeball

DESERT, SIT 12 TO 18 INCHES ABOVE THE GROUND TO STAY

37 "EOD" stands for _____.

(A) Extreme Oceangoing Diver
(B) Explosive Ordnance Disposal
(C) Emergency Operating Device
(D) Extended Olfactory Distress

38 "EPIRB" stands for _____.

(A) Emergency Protective Insulating Radiation Bodysuit
(B) Emergency Police Initial Response Battalion
(C) Extensible Primary Ignition Resistance Baton
(D) Emergency Position Indicating Radio Beacon

39 An elevator shaft is technically known as a
_____.

(A) Shaft way
(B) Hoist way
(C) Straightway
(D) Airway

40 When a plane flies into the wind, the wind is known as a
_____.

(A) Headwind
(B) Tailwind
(C) Fore wind
(D) Front wind

41 The front of a horse's saddle is called the
_____.

(A) Front piece
(B) Cap
(C) Horn
(D) Handle

42 "Stemming" is a technique used in _____.

(A) Sailing
(B) Rock climbing
(C) Bullfighting
(D) Cherry picking

43 In the operation of a fire extinguisher, the acronym
"PASS" stands for _____.

(A) Point Aim Squeeze Squirt
(B) Point And Shoot Straight
(C) Point And Start Spraying
(D) Pull Aim Squeeze Sweep

44 "Trioxane" is a(n) _____.

(A) Portable chemical heat source
(B) Antibiotic ointment
(C) Blood coagulant
(D) Three-stage rocket propellant

WORLD STRIKE THE UNITED STATES . . . A HAILSTONE MEASURING

45 "Anaerobic" bacteria have an aversion to
_____.

(A) Flesh
(B) Air
(C) Water
(D) Exercise

46 A "breech" baby is a baby that _____.
(A) Is turned sideways in the womb
(B) Is too far up the birth canal
(C) Is positioned feet-first in the womb
(D) Is positioned face up in the womb

47 The true name for "killer" bees is _____.
(A) Mexican bees
(B) Brownsville bees
(C) Portuguese bees
(D) Africanized bees

48 On an airplane radio, 121.5 is the _____.
(A) Pilot-to-pilot channel
(B) Emergency channel
(C) Pilot-to-tower channel
(D) Pilot-to-ground control channel

49 A "solenoid" can be found in _____.

(A) A car
(B) The inner ear
(C) A shark's jaws
(D) A bear's claw

50 The femoral artery can be found in the _____.

(A) Heart
(B) Arm
(C) Leg
(D) Stomach

1 (B) **Keys are to escaping from a frozen lake as stout pole is to** floating on quicksand.
Place the pole under your hips to help you float on the quicksand, then slowly make your way to dry land.

2 (A) **Shark is to blood as bear is to** garbage.
Bears have a keen sense of smell and are attracted to human refuse from great distances.

3 (B) **Water is to desert as warm clothing is to** mountains.
Hypothermia is the primary concern when lost in the mountains. Clothing should be layered, with a thin breathable layer next to the skin and two additional layers on top of it.

4 (A) **Tornado is to basement as tsunami is to** tall building.
If you cannot get to higher ground, move to a high floor of a tall building when a tsunami is approaching.

5 (C) **Lyme disease is to tick as rabies is to** raccoon.
Raccoons are one of the primary carriers of rabies, although bats and other small mammals may also be carriers.

6 (A) **Swimming at low tide is to sharks as swimming at dawn is to** piranhas.
Most piranha species sleep at night and feed at dawn.

7 (B) **Eyes and nose are to alligator as eyes and gills are to** shark.
The eyes and gills of a shark are its most sensitive areas and should be the primary targets of your strikes if the shark is attacking you.

STRIKE LAND RATHER THAN WATER . . . ADULT KODIAK BEARS ARE

8 (C) **Rolling like a log is to jumping from a moving train as rolling in a somersault is to** jumping from a car with no brakes.
When leaping out of a moving car, curl up in a ball, protect your head, and roll in a somersault when you hit the ground.

9 (A) **Coat hanger is to locked car door as kicking is to** locked house door.
Giving a few well-placed kicks to the lock area is the best strategy for breaking down a door.

10 (B) **Fingernail is to leech as tweezers are to** tick.
Always use tweezers (or the edges of two credit cards, if tweezers are not available) to remove a tick; never squeeze it or try to burn it off.

11 (A) **Crawling is to volcanic eruption as struggling is to** quicksand.
The viscosity of quicksand increases with shearing, so limit sharp, fast movements; struggling will only make escape more difficult.

12 (A) **Warm water is to frostbite as direct pressure is to** head wound.
Use direct pressure to stop bleeding before moving a victim with a head wound.

13 (B) **Sharing a parachute is to skydiving as sharing a regulator is to** SCUBA diving.
If your air runs out, it is usually better to share a regulator with another diver than to attempt a fast swim to the surface, which may cause an embolism.

14 (A) **Wet towels are to hotel fire as bandanna is to** sandstorm.

THE LARGEST LIVING LAND CARNIVORE AND CAN BE NINE FEET

Place a bandanna over your nose and mouth to keep your airway clear during a sandstorm.

15 (D) **Radio is to plane out of control as fire is to** lost in the wilderness.
Fire is the best method to alert rescuers when you are lost. Build three small, smoky fires during the day, in the shape of a triangle.

16 (C) **Lying flat is to plummeting elevator as standing tall is to** mountain lion.
To deter an attack, stand tall and open your coat wide to appear larger; if a child is present, pick him up and put him on your shoulders.

17 (A) **Spear is to fish as snare is to** rodent.
Wire snares are an excellent way to capture small rodents; place traps on well-used animal tracks or near holes or burrows, and check them regularly.

18 (B) **Eyes are to bird attack as neck is to** mountain lion attack.
Mountain lions tend to attack the neck of their prey, seeking to break the neck or inflict a fatal wound.

19 (A) **Sandbars often trap** sharks **at low tide.**
Sharks may be trapped at low tide between sandbars and the beach, making swimming in these areas especially dangerous.

20 (C) **Liquor is a good thing to offer a corrupt border official.**
Liquor is valued by most cultures, and good brands may be expensive and difficult to obtain in some countries. Offer the liquor as a "sample," not an overt bribe.

TALL . . . MAUNA KEA, AN INACTIVE VOLCANO IN HAWAII, IS

21 (A) **Avoid swimming in the ocean with** shiny jewelry.
Sharks are attracted to light reflecting off shiny jewelry, which may resemble fish scales.

22 (B) **Mountain streams are never home to** piranhas.
Piranhas are only found in slow-moving rivers, backwaters, or floodplain lakes.

23 (D) **A defibrillator is used to treat failure of the** heart.
A defibrillator should be used for victims experiencing sudden cardiac arrest.

24 (B) **During a thunderstorm, it is best to avoid** standing under a lone tree.
If you must seek cover and no true shelter is available, pick a low tree or bush surrounded by taller trees.

25 (C) **A snake will generally strike from a** coiled **position.**
While it is not an absolute rule (a surprised snake may attack from any position), a snake preparing to bite will be coiled or partially coiled to allow a fast, powerful striking movement.

26 (C) **"CPR" stands for** Cardiopulmonary Resuscitation.
CPR should be performed immediately on victims in cardiac arrest; the few minutes before an ambulance arrives can mean the difference between life and death.

27 (B) **The true meaning of "tsunami" is** harbor wave.
Tsunamis are unrelated to the tides, and most are caused by earthquakes.

28 (C) **A Quin-Zhee is also known as a** snow shelter.
A Quin-Zhee offers the same protection from the elements as an igloo but is faster and easier to construct.

33,465 FEET HIGH, TALLER THAN MOUNT EVEREST, IF MEASURED

29 (B) **A "yoke" on the airplane is the** steering wheel.
The yoke, in conjunction with the throttle and flaps, is used
to make changes in a plane's heading and altitude.

30 (C) **"Ion mobility spectroscopy" is used to** detect
explosives.
Ion mobility spectroscopy, now used in many airport security
systems, examines charged molecules to see if they match those
common to illegal drugs and certain explosives.

31 (B) **Your "obliques" can be found in your** abdomen.
When taking a punch to the gut, it is advisable to turn to the
side slightly and absorb the blow with your oblique muscles,
rather than the middle of your abdomen.

32 (A) *Carcharodon carcharias* **is also known as a** white shark.
White sharks, which may be more than 20 feet long, have his-
torically attacked humans more than any other shark species.

33 (B) **Ducques (pronounced "ducks") are** piles of rocks.
Ducques are often used to mark trailheads and by hikers to
denote particular paths or sights of interest.

34 (A) **"Saltation" is** the bouncing movement of small particles, like grains of sand.
Saltation occurs during a sandstorm, when grains of sand
actually bounce as they move.

35 (D) **A "riptide" is more accurately called a** rip current.
Rip currents may be hundreds of feet long but can be escaped
by swimming parallel to the shore.

36 (C) **"Hirudiniasis" occurs when** a leech invades a
body orifice.

FROM THE OCEAN FLOOR TO ITS SUMMIT . . . USING A BUNGEE-

If a leech blocks the airway, it can be dislodged by gargling with high-proof alcohol.

37 (B) **"EOD" stands for** Explosive Ordnance Disposal.
Soldiers who remove land mines are often identified by the acronym "EOD."

38 (D) **"EPIRB" stands for** Emergency Position Indicating Radio Beacon.
Sailors should carry an EPIRB in case of emergency, which will help the Coast Guard determine their exact location.

39 (B) **An elevator shaft is technically known as a** hoist way.
The hoist way contains the elevator car, sometimes called the cabin.

40 (A) **When a plane flies into the wind, the wind is known as a** headwind.
Headwinds slow a flight and cause higher fuel consumption.

41 (C) **The front of a horse's saddle is called the** horn.
The horn of the saddle can be held to maintain balance on uneven terrain.

42 (B) **"Stemming" is a technique used in** rock climbing.
In stemming, climbers push their legs outward against two opposing rock faces and move upward slowly.

43 (D) **In the operation of a fire extinguisher, the acronym "PASS" stands for** Pull Aim Squeeze Sweep.
When using a fire extinguisher, pull the pin, aim the nozzle, squeeze the trigger, then sweep back and forth at the base of the fire.

JUMPING CORD DESIGNED FOR A LIGHTER-WEIGHT JUMPER CAN

44 (A) **"Trioxane" is a** portable chemical heat source. Trioxane is often used by hikers and soldiers for heating precooked, packaged foods.

45 (B) **"Anaerobic" bacteria have an aversion to** air. Anaerobic bacteria may cause infection in head and neck wounds.

46 (C) **A "breech" baby is a baby that** is positioned feet-first in the womb. Though a breech baby may be delivered safely, it is generally preferable for the baby's head to exit the womb first.

47 (D) **The true name for "killer" bees is** Africanized bees. Though Africanized bees rarely kill humans, they are more aggressive than standard honeybees and may kill livestock.

48 (B) **On an airplane radio, 121.5 is the** emergency channel. This channel should be used if there is no response to an emergency call on another channel.

49 (A) **A "solenoid" can be found in** a car. A solenoid is a small, electrically charged coil that produces a magnetic charge.

50 (C) **The femoral artery can be found in the** leg. The femoral artery is a continuation of the aorta. If it is nicked or cut, death by hemorrage may result.

BE FATAL . . . TAKING A BULLET TO THE STOMACH LEAVES A

45 to 50

MASTER. You are ready for anything; your base of survival knowledge is virtually complete. Feel free to head for the world's most dangerous places—adventure awaits!

40 to 44

RANGER. You are well-informed and extremely capable of surviving in most situations. You can head out into the wild as long as you're well equipped.

35 to 39

SCOUT. You have a decent foundation of survival knowledge but could use a bit more training. Go ahead and explore nature and the world—just make sure you've got a guide.

34 and below

BAIT. You are an accident waiting to happen. Try not to leave the house.

HIGHER CHANCE OF SURVIVAL THAN TAKING IT TO THE BACK

EXPERTS AND SOURCES

The American Heart Association

The American Red Cross First Aid and Safety Book, by the American Red Cross and Kathleen A. Handal

Meri-K Appy is vice president for public education at the nonprofit National Fire Protection Association.

The Arizona State Association of 4 Wheel Drive Clubs

Tom Armstrong, a locomotive engineer since 1977, has served as accident prevention coordinator for the Canadian Pacific Railway.

George Arrington, self-defense instructor and teacher of self-defense for more than 25 years, is a fourth-degree black belt and a licensed instructor of Danzan-Ryu Jujutsu.

Eddie Bernard, Ph.D., is director of the Pacific Marine Environmental Laboratory and director of the Pacific Tsunami Warning Center.

Brad Binder, Ph.D., is vice president of W. R. Associates (a security firm based in Wisconsin), as well as a self-defense and assault prevention teacher and private investigator.

The Book of Survival, by Anthony Greenburg

Charles D. Bortle, BA, RRT, NREMT-P, is a paramedic and GMS educator.

Joseph Brennan is the author of *The Guide to Abandoned Subway Stations (Disused or Unused Underground Railway Stations of the New York Area).*

Steve Brill is the author of *Identifying and Harvesting Edible and Medicinal Plants in Wild (and Not-So-Wild) Places.*

Harold Brooks is head of the Mesoscale Applications Group of the National Severe Storms Laboratory.

Dr. Robert Budman ("The Surf Doctor") is an American Board of Family Practice–certified physician and *Surfer* magazine's medical advisor.

George H. Burgess is director of the International Shark Attack File at the Florida Museum of Natural History at the University of Florida.

Robert Cabral is a self-defense instructor and founder of the International Academy of Martial Arts in West Los Angeles.

The California Surf Life-Saving Association

Car Talk is a weekly radio program about car repair broadcast on National Public Radio hosted by Tom and Ray Magliozzi.

Christopher Caso is a stuntman who has produced and performed high-fall stunts for numerous movies, including *Batman and Robin, Batman Forever, The Lost World,* and *The Crow: City of Angels.*

Centers for Disease Control and Prevention

Vince Christopher is a physical therapist and amateur weight lifter in New York.

Tom Claytor, bush pilot, is a fellow of the Explorers Club, a subject of the National Geographic special *Flight over Africa,* and recipient of the Rolex Award for Enterprise.

coldoceans.com

Coleman Cooney is director of the Bullfight School.

Tom Costello is a district manager of Hewlett-Packard.

Paul Cripps is the director of Amazonas Explorer, an organization specializing in adventure travel in Peru and Bolivia.

Danger! Thin Ice, a publication of the Minnesota Department of Natural Resources

Delta Airlines

The Desert Survival Guide, a publication of the City of Phoenix, Arizona

Graham Dickson is a Professional Association of Diving Instructors (PADI) master SCUBA instructor.

David Elwood is a third-degree black belt and Total Approach Jeet Kune Do instructor in the Total Approach Organization headed by Master Leo Fong.

The Erie County (PA) Department of Health

Federal Emergency Management Agency

Janette E. Fennell is founder of TRUNC (Trunk Releases Urgently Needed Coalition; www.netkitchen.com/trunc), a nonprofit whose mission is to make sure children and adults trapped in trunks can escape safely.

Craig Ferreira is a board member of Cape Town's South African White Shark Research Institute.

Tom Flanagan ("The Amazing Flanagan") is a magician and escape artist.

Jim Frankenfield is director of the Cyberspace Snow and Avalanche Center, an Oregon-based nonprofit organization dedicated to avalanche safety education and information.

Greg Gaffney is a veteran of the Naples, Florida, police force and an avid fence climber.

Philip Gee runs Explore the Outback, a safari group that leads nature tours of Australia on camelback.

The Geological Society of America

Brady Geril is vice president of product management for the Counter Spy Shops, the retail division of CCS International Ltd. of London, and former supervising officer and undercover agent in the New York Police Department's narcotics division.

Dale Gibson is a stuntman, teacher of sword-fighting skills to Hollywood actors and stunt people, and sword-fighting stuntman in *The Mask of Zorro*.

Thomas E. Gill is adjunct professor in the Department of Geosciences and a research associate at the Wind Engineering Research Center of Texas Tech University.

Mary Taylor Gray is a writer for *Colorado's Wildlife Company*, a publication of the Colorado Division of Wildlife.

Michael Griffin (www.escapeguy.com) has escaped from prison cells, steel coffins, and from 25 pounds of chains and locks at the bottom of the Pacific Ocean.

Michael Hackenberger runs the Bowmanville Zoological Park in Ontario and has bred and trained lions for 20 years.

Julie Harmon, Ph.D., is executive director of IMPACT Safety Programs, a nonprofit antiviolence organization.

Susan Carol Hauser is the author of *Outwitting Poison Ivy: How to Prevent and Treat the Effects of Poison Ivy, Poison Oak, and Poison Sumac*.

Heartstream

Dr. Jeff Heit, M.D., is director of internal medicine at a Philadelphia-area hospital.

Dr. Peter Henderson is the director of Pisces Conservation Ltd. in Lymington, England.

John Henkel is a writer for the U.S. Food and Drug Administration and a contributor to *FDA Consumer* magazine.

Dave Hill is a UK-based food industry consultant who advises manufacturers and caterers on safe food production.

Larry Holt is a senior consultant at Elcon Elevator Controls and Consulting.

Ron Hood, survival expert, received early wilderness training while he was a member of the U.S. Army and taught wilderness survival classes for 20 years.

The International Tsunami Information Center

Andrew P. Jenkins, Ph.D., WEMT, is professor of community health and physical education at Central Washington University.

Joe Jennings is a skydiving cinematographer and skydiving coordination specialist who has designed, coordinated, and filmed skydiving stunts for numerous television commercials, including Mountain Dew, Pepsi, MTV Sports, Coca-Cola, and ESPN.

Kim Kahana is a stuntman, stunt director, and filmmaker who has appeared in more than 300 films, including *Lethal Weapon 3*, *Passenger 57*, and *Smokey and the Bandit*.

Chris Kallio is the backpacking guide for About.com.

Lynn Kirkland is the curator of the St. Augustine (Florida) Alligator Farm.

Cappy Kotz is a USA Boxing–certified coach and instructor and author of *Boxing for Everyone*.

Karl S. Kruszelnicki is Julius Summer Miller Fellow at the School of Physics of the University of Sydney, Australia, and author of several books on physics and natural phenomena, including *Flying Lasers, Robofish, Cities of Slime, and Other Brain-Bending Science Moments*.

Jeffrey A. Lee is an associate professor in the Department of Economics and Geography at Texas Tech University.

Dr. James Li, practitioner in the Division of Emergency Medicine at Harvard Medical School, is an instructor for the American College of Surgeons course for physicians, Advanced Trauma Life Support.

The Lightning Safety Group of the American Meteorological Society

John Lindner, director of the Wilderness Survival School for the Colorado Mountain Club, is director of training for the Snow Operations Training Center.

John Linstrom is executive director of the Fire and Emergency Television Network, which provides training, information, and education for 240,000 emergency personnel via satellite, videotape, and the Internet.

Jon Lloyd is adventure consultant with VLM Adventure Consultants in the United Kingdom.

David M. Lowell is a certified master locksmith and education/proficiency registration program manager of the Associated Locksmiths of America, an industry trade group.

Christopher Macarak is a kayak instructor and owner of Paddle Trax Kayak Shop in Crested Butte, Colorado.

John Markel is the operator of Midnight Sun Locations, a film and television stunt, location, and safety–consulting firm based in Girdwood, Alaska.

The Martin County (Florida) Board of County Commissioners Information Technology Services

Michael Martinez is a professional tree climber and owner of Specialized Rigging and Tree Care, Inc.

Arthur Marx, a flight instructor, has been a pilot for more than 20 years and owns Flywright Aviation, a flight training and corporate flying service on Martha's Vineyard.

Antonio J. Mendez is a retired CIA intelligence officer and the author of *The Master of Disguise: My Secret Life in the CIA.*

John and Kristy Milchick, horse trainers, own and manage Hideaway Stables in Kentucky.

Chris Mills is a lieutenant in the Philadelphia Fire Department.

Vinny Minchillo, demolition derby driver, is a writer for a variety of automobile magazines, including *AutoWeek, SportsCar,* and *Turbo.*

The National Earthquake Information Center

The National Institute of Allergy and Infectious Diseases

The National Oceanic and Atmospheric Administration

The National Park Service, U.S. Department of the Interior

The National Severe Storms Laboratory

The National Tsunami Hazard Mitigation Program

The National Weather Service Forecast Office, Denver/Boulder, Colorado

The National Weather Service Forecast Office, Miami, Florida

Glen Needham, Ph.D., is co-director of the Ohio State University Acarology Laboratory.

Jim Nishimine, M.D., is an obstetrician and gynecologist at Alta Bates Hospital in Berkeley, California.

The NOAA Tsunami Research Program

The Office of Meteorology, National Weather Service

Gareth Patterson, author and environmentalist, has dedicated most of his adult life to the preservation of the African lion and its wilderness home.

Mike Perrin, co-owns Randall's Adventure and Training, a service that guides extreme expeditions and facilitates training in the jungles of Central America and the Amazon Basin of Peru.

Jay Preston, CSP, PE, is a general safety engineering consultant, forensic safety engineering specialist, and former president of the Los Angeles Chapter of the American Society of Safety Engineers.

Lawrence Price is an auto mechanic and conversion van specialist. He received the Under Construction Class Award at the East Coast Nationals Custom Car Show in 1998 and 1999.

Jeff Randall, survival expert, co-owns Randall's Adventure and Training, a service that guides extreme expeditions and facilitates training in the jungles of Central America and the Amazon Basin of Peru.

The chief consultant (who must remain anonymous) of Real World Rescue, a small, high-risk travel security company based in San Diego, California, that trains elite U.S. government special operations personnel and federal law enforcement agents on international terrorism and Third World survival.

Dr. Lynn Rogers is a wildlife research biologist at Minnesota's Wildlife Research Institute and director of the North American Bear Center in Ely, Minnesota.

Roger Rosen, M.D., is a general practitioner who lives in Philadelphia.

Scott Rowland, Ph.D., is a volcanologist and publisher of the Hawaii Center for Volcanology newsletter.

"Safety Guide to Bears in the Wild," a publication of the Wildlife Branch of Canada's Ministry of Environment, Lands, and Parks

The SAS Survival Driver's Handbook, by John "Lofty" Wiseman

The SAS Survival Handbook, by John "Lofty" Wiseman

Greta Schanen is managing editor of *Sailing* magazine.

Dr. David Schleser, researcher and eco-travel guide, is the author of *Piranhas: Everything about Selection, Care, Nutrition, Diseases, Breeding, and Behavior (More Complete Pet Owner's Manuals)*.

Stanley A. Schultz, president of the American Tarantula Society, is the author of the *Tarantula Keeper's Guide,* 2nd edition.

Mark E. Siddall is assistant curator for the Division of Invertebrate Zoology at the American Museum of Natural History in New York City.

Thomas W. Simons, a former U.S. ambassador to Pakistan, and his wife, Margaret

Tim Smalley is boating and water safety education coordinator for the Minnesota Department of Natural Resources.

The Society for the Preservation of Alien Contact Evidence and Geographic Exploration (SPACEAGE)

Jean-Philippe Soule, leader of the Central American Sea Kayak Expedition 2000, is a former member of the elite French Mountain Commando unit.

Patty Sprott is an ecologist who disseminates scientific findings of the Long Term Ecological Research Network, a National Science Foundation–funded program.

Scott Stockwell is a U.S. Army major, combat medical entomologist, and consultant on scorpion envenomation.

Barry Tedder is a marine biologist and jungle survival expert.

The Texas Agricultural Extension Service

The Texas Parks & Wildlife Department

Janet Tobiassen, DVM, is a small-animal veterinarian and the veterinary medicine guide at About.com.

Sam Toler is an auto mechanic, demolition derby driver, and member of the Internet Demolition Derby Association.

Jon Turk is the author of *Cold Oceans: Adventures in Kayak, Rowboat, and Dogsled*.

United Airlines

The U.S. Army Medical Research and Materiel Command

The U.S. Army Survival Manual

The U.S. Army's Cold Regions Research and Engineering Laboratory, Hanover, New Hampshire

The U.S. Geological Survey

The U.S. State Department

Jack Viorel is a teacher who has lived and worked throughout Central and South America.

William Waldock is a professor of Aeronautical Science at Embry-Riddle Aeronautical University and has completed more than 75 field investigations and over 200 accident analyses.

John Wehbring is a mountaineering instructor, a member of the San Diego Mountain Rescue Team, a former chairman of the Mountain Rescue Association (California region), and a teacher of the Sierra Club's Basic Mountaineering course.

Mike Wilbanks is webmaster of Constrictors.com.

Tim Williams is a lecturer and trainer of alligator wrestlers at Gatorland.

Mick Wilson is the author of *How to Crash an Airplane (and Survive!)*. He has a gold seal flight instructor certificate for both single- and multi-engine aircraft.

Jim Winburn is the director and stunt coordinator for two amusement park shows: "Batman Action Show" and "The Further Adventure of Butch Cassidy and the Sundance Kid."

David L. Ziegler is president of Ziegler & Associates, a security consulting firm concentrating on fire and arson investigation.

Al Zulich is director of the Harford Reptile Breeding Center in Bel Air, Maryland.

ABOUT THE AUTHORS

Joshua Piven knows that not all questions have answers, not all answers have questions, and some questions are, without question, unanswerable (or something like that). He is the co-author, with David Borgenicht, of the *Worst-Case Scenario Survival Handbook* series.

David Borgenicht is a) the co-author, with Joshua Piven, of all of the books in the bestselling *Worst-Case Scenario Survival Handbook* series, b) the publisher of Quirk Books, a Philadelphia-based book publisher, c) a father of two and husband (of one), d) a guy who once stowed away on Amtrak, e) all of the above. ANSWER: E

Brenda Brown is an illustrator and cartoonist whose work has been published in many books and publications, including *The Worst-Case Scenario Survival Handbook* series, *Esquire, Reader's Digest, USA Weekend, 21st Century Science & Technology, The Saturday Evening Post,* and *The National Enquirer.* Her website is http://webtoon.com.

THE FIRST OF THE WORST

The
WORST-CASE SCENARIO
Survival Handbook

HOW TO:
→ Escape from Quicksand
→ Wrestle an Alligator
→ Break Down a Door
→ Land a Plane . . .

By Joshua Piven and David Borgenicht

⚠ 3 million copies
in print

⚠ Translated into
27 languages

⚠ International
bestseller

"An armchair guide for
the anxious."
—*USA Today*

"The book to have when the
killer bees arrive."
—*The New Yorker*

"Nearly 180 pages of immediate action drills for when
everything goes to hell in
a handbasket."
—*Soldier of Fortune*

"This is a really nifty book."
—*Forbes*

A BOOK FOR EVERY DISASTER

The Worst-Case Scenario Survival Handbook

The Worst-Case Scenario Survival Handbook: Travel

The Worst-Case Scenario Survival Handbook: Dating & Sex

The Worst-Case Scenario Survival Handbook: Golf

The Worst-Case Scenario Survival Handbook: Holidays

The Worst-Case Scenario Survival Handbook: Work

The Worst-Case Scenario Survival Handbook: College

The Worst-Case Scenario Survival Handbook: Weddings

The Worst-Case Scenario Survival Handbook: Parenting